"Imagine Paul preaching in first-century Athens. Now imagine stepping into Paul's shoes and proclaiming the gospel in the twenty-first-century Western world. In this thought-provoking book, a Christian apologist and a New Testament scholar join forces to read Luke's famous story of Paul on Mars Hill, and the result is as compelling as it is remarkable. Copan and Litwak issue a robust invitation for God's people to read Scripture and our increasingly post-Christian world together in the service of communicating well the good news."

Joel B. Green, professor of New Testament interpretation, Fuller Theological Seminary

"Nuanced and well-informed on the biblical evidence, this book offers a sound biblical model for communicating Christian faith in engaging ways today. It rightly understands Paul's Areopagus speech as a model, and translates that speech's approach into analogous forms for our culture."

Craig Keener, author of *The IVP Bible Background Commentary: New Testament*

"Copan and Litwak have produced a brilliant book that sheds light on the dynamic, turbulent intellectual climate that Paul faced in ancient Athens. They demonstrate why Paul's teaching is as important and powerful in the twenty-first century as it was in the first century."

Charles Taliaferro, professor of philosophy, St. Olaf College

The *The* GOSPEL
in the
MARKETPLACE
of IDEAS

PAUL'S MARS HILL EXPERIENCE
for OUR PLURALISTIC WORLD

Paul Copan *and*
Kenneth D. Litwak

IVP Academic

An imprint of InterVarsity Press
Downers Grove, Illinois

InterVarsity Press
P.O. Box 1400, Downers Grove, IL 60515-1426
World Wide Web: www.ivpress.com
Email: email@ivpress.com

InterVarsity Press® is the book-publishing division of InterVarsity Christian Fellowship/USA®, a movement of students and faculty active on campus at hundreds of universities, colleges and schools of nursing in the United States of America, and a member movement of the International Fellowship of Evangelical Students. For information about local and regional activities, write Public Relations Dept., InterVarsity Christian Fellowship/USA, 6400 Schroeder Rd., P.O. Box 7895, Madison, WI 53707-7895, or visit the IVCF website at www.intervarsity.org.

Cover design: David Fassett
Interior design: Beth Hagenberg

Images: newspaper tears: © tjhunt/iStockphoto
*   Paul the Apostle illustration: © pictore/iStockphoto*
*   Time Square at night: © Mlenny/iStockphoto*

ISBN 978-0-8308-4043-4 (print)
ISBN 978-0-8308-8409-4 (digital)

Printed in the United States of America ♾

Library of Congress Cataloging-in-Publication Data

Copan, Paul.
The gospel in the marketplace of ideas : Paul's Mars Hill experience for
our pluralistic world / Paul Copan and Kenneth D. Litwak.
*   pages cm*
Includes bibliographical references and index.
ISBN 978-0-8308-4043-4 (pbk. : alk. paper)
1. Bible. Acts, XVII, 16-34—Criticism, interpretation, etc. 2. Paul,
the Apostle, Saint. 3. Athens (Greece)—Religion. 4. Christianity and
other religions. 5. Evangelistic work. 6. Apologetics. 7. Witness
bearing (Christianity) 8. Missions. I. Title.
BS2625.52.C67 2014
226.6'06--dc23

*   2014012495*

P	21	20	19	18	17	16	15	14	13	12	11	10	9	8	7	6	5	4	3	2	1
Y	32	31	30	29	28	27	26	25	24	23	22	21	20	19	18	17	16	15	14		

From Ken

To Amanda, my beloved wife,
who truly fits her name,
and to our sons,
Matthew, Wesley and Daniel

From Paul

To my dear son Jonathan,
who loves and cares for others,
is full of creativity and initiative,
and shows much promise as a
servant in God's kingdom

CONTENTS

ABBREVIATIONS

Descr.	Pausanias, *Graeciae description*
Ep.	Seneca, *Epistulae morales*
Epict. diss.	Arrian, *Epicteti dissertationes*
Eum.	Aeschylus, *Eumenides*
Gen. litt.	Augustine, *On Genesis Literally Interpreted*
Her.	Ovid, *Heroides*
Hist.	Thucydides, *Historia*
LXX	Septuagint
Off.	Cicero, *De officiis*
Rep.	Cicero, *De republica*
Rhet. Her.	Pseudo-Cicero, *Rhetorica ad Herennium*
Sat.	Petronius, *Satyricon*
Vit.	Diogenes Laertius, *Vita philosophorum*
Vit. Apoll.	Philostratus, *Vita Apollonii*

Welcome to Athens

We live in a multicultural world with many races and ethnic groups. To add to this already interesting mix, there are a huge number of religious and philosophical beliefs, from the monotheism of Judaism, to the do-it-yourself New Age spirituality or the strident New Atheism, to the "I don't care" attitude of apatheism. At least in the Western world, there are so many religious and philosophical ideas that it is hard to know about, much less fully understand, them all.

Western culture has begun to resemble the relativism repeatedly described in the book of Judges: "Everyone did was what right in his [or her] own eyes" (Judg 21:25 NASB). To say that the basic Judeo-Christian ethic that has generally served as the basis for law in the Western world has been in many ways discarded is an understatement. The situation in which we find ourselves at the beginning of the twenty-first century prompts us to ask, how can we authentically and effectively present the message of Jesus the Messiah to those around us? As we move more and more into a post-Christian age, our neighbors, classmates, coworkers and even extended family members know less and less about what it means to believe in Christ. What they do know is often a caricature gained more from MTV or some television sitcom or from a hostile anti-Christian college professor than from the Bible. How can we communicate to them the truth of the gospel in ways that they can understand?

This is a difficult question, and there are many possible answers. We could throw up our hands in despair at ever reaching those around us because they are hostile to what they think that Christians believe. Others continue to use methods from earlier decades, such as asking people, "If you died tonight, do you know if you would go to heaven?"—a question that is only meaningful if both parties know what heaven is and share some basic premises, such as there being a personal G/god who holds us accountable for our actions. Whether believers are vilified because of the many unchristian things we supposedly or actually say and do, or do not do, or are ignored because "all roads lead to God/salvation," we have a challenge before us if we are to carry out Jesus' last command: Go make disciples among all the nations (Mt 28:19).

Today we are aware that an array of belief systems and social structures exist that differ greatly in their major themes as well as their details. But the same was true in the first-century Mediterranean world. The apostle Paul also lived in and carried out his evangelism in a multicultural setting in the first century. From Jews to Gentiles, elite to poor, slaves and slave owners, many rights for men but few rights for women, olive-skinned Jews or native Ephesian Gentiles to dark-skinned Ethiopians, the Greco-Roman world was a huge mixture of races and ethnic groups. There were many religions practiced —from the imperial cult of emperor worship, to temples for the traditional Greek pantheon, to the secret rituals of the mystery religions—and there

were all manner of theological views. There were devout worshipers of Asclepius, a god of healing, and at the same time a growing trend that held these gods, if they existed at all, to be irrelevant. The Roman Empire was filled with beliefs in evil spirits and magical practices one might use to protect oneself from these spirits. Among some, the ideas about deities were modified as people, not least those in Athens, constructed philosophies to live by and understand the world.

A "worldview" is a philosophy of life that reflects a deeper heart commitment. Everyone has a worldview that attempts to answer questions such as: Why am I here? Why does anything exist at all? What am I to do or think?

Figure 1.1. Asclepius, Apollo's son and the god of medicine, had devout followers since healing from illness and protecting oneself from malevolent spirits were major concerns for many in the first century.

How can my life have meaning? Across the Roman Empire, people attempted to answer these questions by mixing and matching ideas and religious teaching. They grappled with fear of evil spirits, among other things, and generally came up with many "construct your own" worldviews.

When Paul found himself in Athens, it was not primarily to carry out evangelism, but Paul did not waste the opportunity. Grieved by the false religion he saw expressed through temples and idols, Paul went into the main marketplace of Athens and began speaking with anyone who came by and was willing to have a dialogue. It was clear to Paul that these people did not know the true God, while Paul knew himself to have been commissioned by Jesus to proclaim the good news about Jesus to Gentiles. Like many cities to which Paul traveled, Athens had its own unique history. It had been the center of the birth of Greek philosophy. In fact the viewpoints of Plato and Aristotle were so influential that we often still use their ideas as the basis for our intellectual pursuits. For example, the Platonic idea of the immortality of the soul is a common belief even in Christian circles. So is the Platonic notion that the physical world is less real than, and inferior to, the soul and the transcendent realm of the "forms," like justice and goodness. Although some of Plato's ideas have been adapted by such Christian theologians as Augustine to make sense of biblical doctrines like evil and God as "spirit," Plato's views had a negative impact on the early church (the heresy of Gnosticism), which has continued throughout church history and strongly resembles much in Eastern spirituality today. Athens, whatever else it was, was still seen as a center of learning and wisdom in the Greco-Roman world, and we are still feeling its effects.

Paul was knowledgeable about the philosophical and religious beliefs of the Athenians. One prominent Athenian school was Stoicism, founded by Zeno of Cyprus and developed by a later Zeno from Paul's hometown— Tarsus, another of the three great centers of learning in the Roman Empire (the third being Alexandria in Egypt). Paul would have had plenty of opportunity to learn about Stoicism and competing worldviews.

No wonder, then, when Paul was challenged to explain the new foreign gods that the Athenians thought he was proclaiming, he brought together his knowledge of Scripture and Jewish traditions and theology with the practices of Gentile idolaters and philosophers. Paul used their language and quoted their poets in the process of proclaiming the story of God's action in and for the world, though his thinking was grounded in the Hebrew Scriptures. He approached his audience carefully and cordially, perhaps complimenting them on their religious devotion, and told them about the one true God who had demonstrated his concern for and expectations of humans by raising Jesus from the dead, a concept that some of his audience could not handle.

The Acts of the Apostles in the New Testament offers us wise guidance in knowing what to do in response to Jesus' call, and about how to describe God's rescue plan for the once-good, now-damaged creation. Unfortunately, the sermons in the book of Acts wouldn't be readily understood by non-Christians in our secularized culture. If you walk up to someone randomly on a university campus or at the local coffee bar and attempt to reach that person by quoting Bible verses, and the person you are addressing neither knows what's in the Bible nor really cares, or has a faulty image—a caricature—of God that is unpalatable, you will not get any further than someone who speaks only German talking to someone who speaks only Chinese.

In this book, we want to address this "translation" problem head-on. The approach we will take is to look at the background and contents of Paul's speech to the Athenians, which is recorded in Acts 17:16-34. We will look first at the validity of using Paul's example (chapter two). Next, we will examine the cultural, religious and philosophical situation in the physical city of Athens during the first century A.D. (chapter three).

Dominant schools of thought in Paul's day, including Platonism and Epicureanism, have had a lingering influence in Western culture up to the present; so we should examine how Paul engaged with thinkers of his day to help us engage with our own culture. Plato's views led to the unbiblical Christian belief that disembodied souls spend eternity without bodies in heaven. Plato's denigration of the material world, and bodies in particular, led to the Christian view of the body as a prison of the soul instead of the body being God's good creation that will one day be raised to immortality. Learning about Plato and other early Greek philosophers can help us not only understand Paul's speech better but avoid unbiblical teaching. Chapter four will shift to the Athens of today, using *Athens* and *Athenians* metaphorically to refer to people and their cultural, religious, academic, political, philosophical and social context in our own world.

Chapter five describes the nature and role of Paul's speech within the Acts of the Apostles: What was Luke trying to do with this speech? Chapter six describes the religious and philosophical beliefs of the Athenians who would have listened to Paul, followed by chapter seven, which describes the beliefs that Paul as a Jew and a Christian held. Like Paul, we need to know what non-Christians believe and be clear on the truths of the Christian faith and how to express them.

Chapter eight examines Paul's approach to his Athenian audience in detail so that we can see what principles or practices Luke wants us to follow. All this information on Acts 17:16-34, while we think it is interesting in its own right, has one primary aim, namely to give readers the necessary background for approaching today's Athenians in a biblical way. Chapter nine puts this all together by showing how we can do the same sorts of things in our culture as Paul did in his, framing his presentation of what God has done in and through Jesus in ways that would be comprehensible to his audience. Finally, we apply a number of these lessons from Paul to our situation—going to our own Mars Hill—which complements chapter four ("Our Athens").

Some readers might be anxious to get to the modern-day part and not spend time on the historical, religious and philosophical world of Paul's day. Indeed, both of us have had more than one student who has said that their pastor or elder has asserted that no one needs to study the ancient world. All one has to do is read the Bible and that will be enough. If the Bible reader who makes this claim has a thorough grasp of the cultural, social, political, philosophical, religious and linguistic (the person is fluent in Koine Greek) background of the New Testament, to say nothing of the many centuries, peoples, customs, lands and languages relevant to understanding the Old Testament, we would agree fully.

The problem is, we have never met anyone like that, not even a senior biblical scholar. For the rest of us, it's necessary to do some study. If we don't learn about the world in which Paul evangelized, it will be hard to understand his speeches in their original context, and much harder to apply the principles that he used. Consequently, we will spend time digging down into what Luke is doing with the speeches in Acts, Paul's theology that informed his speech in Athens, and the competing beliefs of members of his audience.

That does not mean that you need to prepare for a long, dry history lesson. We have both read more than our fair share of academic books, including very tedious ones. Instead, the following chapters offer readers enough information to understand what Paul is doing in his speech in Athens so that they can follow his example in learning about what non-believers in today's world think in order to shape, not compromise, their presentation of the gospel.

We can no longer rely (if we ever could rely) upon other people understanding our "Christianese," or believing anything other than caricatures of what committed, orthodox Christians believe. We cannot expect unbelievers to learn our ideas first so that they can understand us. We need to go to them, learn what they think and find ways to present them with the truths of the gospel in ways that will be meaningful to them.

All of this is presented in the hopes that you, our readers, will gain practical help in presenting the gospel in your context. This is not a timeless recipe that is being offered by making specific suggestions for today's world and today's Athenians. Rather, we offer patterns and models from which you can learn or that serve as a springboard for exploration in other areas. To some extent, Paul's speech in Athens served to make room on the table for the ideas he was presenting about God. We likewise may need to do some pre-evangelistic table clearing ourselves in order to earn the right to be heard. It is our hope that this book will help give you wisdom in presenting the gospel to today's Athenians.

ACTS 17:16-34

^{16}*And while Paul was waiting for them in Athens, his spirit was being provoked within him when he observed that the city was full of idols.* ^{17}*Therefore, he was arguing in the synagogue with the Jews and God-fearers and in the marketplace every day with those who happened to be present.* ^{18}*And certain people, both of the Epicurean and the Stoic philosophers, were conversing with him, and some were saying, "What might this foolish babbler wish to say?" but others, "He seems to be a proclaimer of strange gods," because he was announcing good news about Jesus and Anastasis.* ^{19}*And after having taken hold of him they led [Paul] to the Areopagus, saying, "May we know what this new teaching is that is being spoken by you?* ^{20}*For you are bringing certain astonishing things into our hearing. Therefore we want to know what these things mean."*

^{21}*Now all the Athenians and foreigners staying there were spending their time in nothing other than (trying) to say something or to hear something new.* ^{22}*And after he stood in the middle of the Areopagus, Paul said, "In every way I see that you are very religious.* ^{23}*For while I was going through [Athens] and looking carefully at your objects of worship, I came upon even an altar on which had been written, 'to an unknown God.' Therefore, that which you, being ignorant of it, worship, this I proclaim to you.*

^{24}*"The God who has made the cosmos and everything that is in it, this one, since he is the Lord of heaven and earth, does not dwell in temples made by human hands,* ^{25}*nor is he served by human hands, as if he needed something, since he himself gives to all life and breath and indeed all things. ²⁶And he made from one person every nation of humankind on the whole face of the earth, having determined fixed times and the boundaries of their dwelling place, ²⁷in order that they might seek God, if perhaps indeed they might grope for and find him, though he is not far away from each one of us. ²⁸For by him we live and do what we do and exist, as some of your own poets have said, 'For we are his offspring.'*

²⁹"Therefore, since we are the offspring of God, we ought not to suppose that the divine nature is like gold or silver or stone, an image made by human skill and thought. ³⁰So although God had formerly disregarded the times of ignorance, now he instructs all people everywhere to repent, ³¹because he has set a day on which he is going to judge the world in righteousness, by a man whom he has appointed, having offered proof to everyone by raising him from the dead." ³²Now when they heard "resurrection from the dead," some began to scoff, but others said, "We would like to hear you concerning this matter again!"

³³So Paul went out from their midst. ³⁴Now some people, having joined him, believed, among whom were also Dionysius, a member of the Areopagus, and a woman named Damaris and others with them.

(Translation by Kenneth D. Litwak.)

Was Paul's Speech at Athens a Mistake?

Paul went to the city of Athens, where there was a hill known in Greek as the *Areopagus*—a rocky hill named for Ares, the Greek god of war. Paul was then brought before the Areopagus. *Areopagus* was used to refer both to a place on a hillside—the "hill of Ares" (or "Mars," the Latin equivalent)—and to a governing body that met at the Areopagus. The word *Areopagus* itself symbolized justice to the Athenians. This Aeropagus, or Mars Hill, was the purported location of the trial of Zeus's son, Ares, before the twelve-god tribunal on Mount Olympus. Zeus's brother Poseidon was suing for justice against Ares, charging him with the murder of his son, Halirrhothius. Nevertheless, Ares was acquitted. The Romans adopted the Greek pantheon of gods and goddesses for themselves but gave them new names. Zeus became Jupiter, Artemis became Diana, and Ares became Mars. Therefore, the Areopagus is sometimes called Mars Hill.[1]

That is one bit of table clearing to be done. But before we can really get on with the journey before us into Paul's Athens and then our own, there is one other bit of table clearing

Figure 2.1. This colossal statue of Mars Ultor (Mars the Avenger) is from the end of the first century A.D.

that is necessary. Some have argued that Paul's approach at Athens was all wrong, but we disagree and find the evidence for this to be shaky at best.

The late evangelical New Testament scholar F. F. Bruce wrote a classic study of the apostle Paul titled *Paul: Apostle of the Heart Set Free*. His biblical commentaries as well as his books on the trustworthiness of the New Testament have been a reliable resource for many Bible-believing Christians; so readers will likely be surprised to read Bruce's negative comments on Paul's Areopagus (Mars Hill) speech in Acts 17. To most Christians, it would appear that Luke, who devotes much space to summarizing Paul's conversation with the Athenians and his speech to them, speaks quite positively about Paul's strategy. After all, he, the narrator himself, gives no hint of disparagement about Paul's approach. Yet Bruce creates a mood of depression and discouragement after Athens: "Paul travelled from Athens to Corinth in a mood of dejection."[2] Paul's attempts had been met with "polite amusement," and the response had been "much less encouraging" than in the cities of Macedonia he had just visited—Philippi, Berea and Thessalonica.[3]

Bruce believed that Paul's preaching had been something of a failure not only in terms of response, but strategy as well. Bruce allows that Paul's speech at Athens was perhaps more of a laying of the groundwork for the gospel rather than directly evangelizing.[4] But Paul was "experimenting with this approach" to Gentile evangelism to discover what would be most effective; so "it is probable that Paul's decision at Corinth [to directly preach 'the word of the cross,' as in 1 Cor 1:18] was based on his assessment of the situation there [at Athens]."[5]

Similarly, the late William Ramsay claimed that Paul—because of the apparently meager response to his Areopagus speech, in which he cited Stoic thinkers for reinforcement—was "disappointed and perhaps disillusioned by his experience in Athens. He felt that he had gone at least as far as was right in the way of presenting his doctrine in a form suited to the current philosophy; and the result had been little more than naught."[6] Another biblical scholar, Ralph P. Martin, asks, "Had Paul failed in this situation?" However, Martin does not answer the question.[7]

So, the argument goes, Paul determined that at his next stop, he wanted to "know nothing" while he was with the Corinthians "but Christ and him crucified" (1 Cor 2:2). At Corinth, Paul would preach "the foolishness" of

Christ crucified, not with "excellence of speech" and human reasoning (cf. 1 Cor 1–2), but by the power and Spirit of God. So, no more philosophical reasoning for Paul! No more quoting of pagan thinkers in an attempt to build bridges with his pagan audience! From now on, he was just going to give people the unvarnished gospel!

But is this what really happened? Does this fairly represent Paul's thinking as portrayed in the book of Acts and in his epistles, particularly 1 Corinthians? In this chapter, we challenge the notion that Paul was not faithfully presenting the gospel and that his approach was a mistaken deviation from his standard gospel preaching. Paul's Areopagus speech truly reflects the heart of Paul's Christ-centered strategy. This approach has important implications for the believers engaging in crosscultural missions. Not only that; it gives key insights into "cross-worldview communication"[8]—the phrase one Christian philosopher uses for apologetics, which attempts to defend the Christian faith in the marketplace of ideas.

Figure 2.2. The Areopagus (Mars Hill) in Athens. This rocky hill was named for Ares, the Greek god of war. Mars, the Roman god of war, is identified with Ares.

Typically, those who oppose Christian apologetics today are more likely to be inside the church than outside. And even if they do not consider Paul's approach wrong-headed, they often consider attempts at cross-worldview communication or apologetics to be detracting from the gospel or somehow adding works to grace (more on this below).

The biblical scholar N. T. Wright observes: "Much Pauline scholarship in the last generations has ignored this [Areopagus] speech."[9] In this book, we want to explore the background, details and implications of this speech for the wisdom it affords us as we connect with today's Athenians in our own culture. But first we want to explore the fundamental question of whether Paul's approach was actually mistaken.

THE WISDOM OF PAUL'S ADDRESS TO THE ATHENIANS

The first response to the charge that Paul made a mistake is that this is an argument from silence. Luke gives no indication of this. In fact, why would he devote so much space to this speech if it was a mistake and Luke said nothing to correct this? If so much of the speech ran contrary to the preaching of the cross, then this could undermine Luke's own theological approach laid out in the book of Acts.

Second, the charge that Paul made a strategic mistake reads into Acts a specific situation at Corinth. How so? In 1 Corinthians, Paul was addressing the congregation's arrogance and spiritual one-upmanship—a complete departure from dependence on the sufficiency of Christ and the power of the Spirit. They had emphasized their giftedness in knowledge and wisdom and rhetoric. They glorified speaking in tongues over other supposedly inferior spiritual gifts. They thought they had arrived: "You have become kings without us," Paul told them (1 Cor 4:8 NASB). They elevated social status so highly that they were willing to tolerate, even boast about, the gross immorality of one of their prominent members (1 Cor 5).[10] And the new covenant blessings through the Spirit overshadowed any need for a future bodily resurrection (1 Cor 15:12). The Corinthians' own skewed theological perspective emphasized the "already" of the blessings God has made available to us in Christ, but they ignored the "not yet" aspect—that the final removal of sin, death and sorrow, as well as the provision of an immortal resurrection body, have not yet been realized. This view is what one scholar has fittingly called "over-realized eschatology."[11] Yes, the Corinthians believed they had all blessings in

Christ—and nothing was left for the new heavens and new earth!

Paul was chiding the Corinthians for their spiritual pride and puffed-up, misguided wisdom. Paul didn't oppose rational argument or the use of the mind. Paul was opposing human pride and self-sufficiency. The word of the cross is folly not because it is irrational or illogical, but it strikes at the heart of human pride and boasting in this-worldly achievements. The foolishness of the cross is not opposed to objective evidence. Those who denigrate philosophy or apologetics based on 1 Corinthians 1–2 need to keep reading to the end of the book! In 1 Corinthians 15, Paul lists the eyewitnesses to the bodily resurrection of Jesus and even tells his readers that most of the five hundred believers who saw Jesus after his resurrection were still alive to be questioned. Paul's emphasis on the foolishness of the cross does not oppose objective evidence and fair-minded investigation. What's more, in the same chapter of the letter to the Corinthians, Paul is still quoting pagans just like he did at Athens! He cites Menander: "Bad company corrupts good character" (1 Cor 15:33 NIV).[12]

Third, Paul's bridge-building approach was much the same before and after Athens. Before Athens, Paul would "reason" with people in an attempt to "persuade" them (Acts 17:2-4). In the synagogue in Thessalonica, he "reasoned with them from the Scriptures" (Acts 17:2 NASB). During his visit to Athens, he "was reasoning" with Jews and God-fearing Gentiles in the synagogue and with pagans who happened to be present "in the market place every day" (Acts 17:17 NASB). Also, Paul continues the same approach after Athens, in both Corinth (Acts 18:4) and Ephesus (Acts 18:19; 19:8-9). In fact, when Paul was forced by hostile Jews to abandon discussions at the Ephesian synagogue, he went to the school of Tyrannus, where he was "reasoning daily" (Acts 19:9 NASB). As a result, Jews and Gentiles alike heard the gospel (Acts 19:10). Paul's reasoning with Jews and pagans alike was undertaken with the same dependence on God's Spirit.

Furthermore, when we compare the content of Paul's message at Athens with his earlier message to pagans at Lystra (Acts 14), we see striking parallels (see table 2.1). What's more, in both messages, Paul expresses the same key theological themes from the Old Testament, including the witness of God in creation.

Table 2.1. Comparison of Paul's Message at Lystra with His Message at Athens

Key Theological Themes	Paul at Lystra: Acts 14:15-17	Paul at Athens: Acts 17:24-30
1. God as creator	"We . . . preach the gospel to you that you should turn from these vain things to a living God, **who made the heaven and the earth and the sea and all that is in them."** (Acts 14:15 NASB)[a]	"The God who made the world and all things in it, since He is Lord of heaven and earth, does not dwell in temples made with hands." (Acts 17:24 NASB)[b]
2. God as life-giver to (nondivine) humans	"We are also men of the same nature as you." (Acts 14:15 NASB)	"He Himself gives to all people life and breath . . . ; and He made from one man every nation of mankind to live on all the face of the earth, having determined their appointed times and the boundaries of their habitation." (Acts 17:25-26 NASB)[c]
3. The witness of God in creation	"And yet He did not leave Himself without witness, in that He did good and gave you rains from heaven and fruitful seasons, satisfying your hearts with food and gladness." (Acts 14:17 NASB)	"He Himself gives to all people life and breath and all things; . . . that they would seek God, if perhaps they might grope for Him and find Him, though He is not far from each one of us." (Acts 17:25, 27 NASB)
4. Previous ignorance	"In the generations gone by He permitted all the nations to go their own ways." (Acts 14:16 NASB)	"Therefore having overlooked the times of ignorance . . ." (Acts 17:30 NASB)
5. Call to repentance	"Turn from these vain things to a living God." (Acts 14:15 NASB)	"Declaring . . . that all people everywhere should repent." (Acts 17:30 NASB)

[a]The boldfaced portion of the Scripture is a quotation from Exodus 20:11/Psalm 146:6 (cf. Neh 9:6).
[b]Interestingly, Stephen uses similar wording in his speech to the Jews earlier in Acts (7:48 NASB): "However, the Most High does not dwell in houses made by human hands."
[c]Here Paul speaks of the varied human cultures throughout the world (Gen 1:28; 9:1, 7; 10:5, 20, 31-32), all under God's rule.

Paul used the same basic approach in both places. In fact, at Athens he even had opportunity to mention Jesus and his resurrection. This was more than he was able to do at Lystra, where his sermon was interrupted by a mob dragging him out of the city and stoning him (Acts 14:19)![13] In Acts 21, Paul's speech to Jewish people would result in a riot in Jerusalem. All in all, Paul fared quite well in Athens by comparison.

Fourth, we should not miss Luke's clear point that Paul is proclaiming the gospel to the Athenians. Luke refers to the gospel as "the word of God" throughout Acts; that is, this is the same message of Jesus (in Luke) and his messengers (in Acts). As in the parable of the sower and the seed, the seed is called the "word of God" (Lk 8:8), which Luke describes elsewhere as the message of Jesus himself (Lk 5:2). This "word" that is sown (proclaimed) multiplies and bears much fruit throughout the book of Acts (5:31; 6:7; 12:24; 13:7, 15, 44, 46, 48, 49; 19:20). Paul's speech at Athens is no exception to the proclaimed "word" bearing fruit. In fact, in Acts 17:18, we're told that Paul is preaching the good news about "Jesus and the resurrection" (NIV). From start to finish, Luke makes clear, Paul's proclamation in Athens is quite in line with the good news announced by Jesus himself.[14]

Fifth, Paul's approach in Athens merely illustrates yet another Corinthians passage—that Paul, more than Jesus' disciples, was quite able to contextualize the gospel for Jew and Gentile alike. Paul declared himself a slave of all so that he might win some—a Jew to the Jew and a Gentile to the Gentiles, who were "without the law" of Moses (1 Cor 9:19-27).

The biblical scholar N. T. Wright points out that Paul inhabited three worlds:[15]

- Second Temple Judaism with its critique of pagan idolatry and oppressive empires

- Hellenism, which, thanks to Alexander the Great, passed on the Greek language and culture, including a Greek philosophical outlook

- Roman Empire, of which Paul was a citizen and which had its ideology and cult of emperor worship

A fourth world could be added—the realm of the Messiah: being part of a new humanity, family and community "in Christ" gave shape to a new identity for Paul. Thus, we could say that Paul's Christian faith was "rooted in Judaism, lived out in the Hellenistic world, and placing a counter-claim against Caesar's aspiration to world domination."[16]

Being the cosmopolitan man he was, Paul adapted to his audiences. For one thing, he was in the upper 1 to 2 percent of the educated people of his day.[17] Because of his background, being from Tarsus ("a citizen of no insignificant city," Acts 21:39 NASB), he could speak to cultural elites. Yet Paul had also studied under the esteemed rabbi Gamaliel I (Acts 22:3). Being a Tarsian, a well-educated Jew and a Roman citizen were quite significant for Paul's ministry to the Gentiles. He was a remarkably well-credentialed man (2 Cor 11:21-22; Phil 3:4-6). Not surprisingly, God used Paul's wide-ranging background to bring the gospel to the Gentiles in cultural centers such as Athens, Corinth and Ephesus. Unlike the Galilean apostles, who would work primarily with the circumcised (Gal 2:9), Paul's background furnished him with "a broader view of Jews and Greeks, women and men, slaves and free persons . . . than would be the case if he had been raised in a cultural backwater somewhere in the rural parts of the Holy Land."[18]

On his missionary journeys, Paul's strategy began with the familiar Jewish synagogues. These became crucial beachheads for Paul. He would typically begin with synagogue-goers, of whom a good number turned to Christ. These converts in turn would proclaim the good news to their pagan neighbors. But when Paul encountered pagans directly, as at Lystra and Athens, his message was anchored in the Old Testament and did not deviate from the gospel he proclaimed to the Jews. No, Paul's approach at Athens was not a method he decided to scrap once he arrived at Corinth. Rather, his speech at Athens, something of an expanded version of the speech he gave at Lystra, was both insightful and culturally sensitive. His message was properly anchored in a robust monotheism centered on the saving work of Jesus of Nazareth as God's agent in the world.

Paul's experience and speech at Athens were no theological or evangelistic aberration. Rather, they serve as a model for imitation in communicating the gospel crossculturally. Having cleared the table of this potential objection, we can begin to explore the Athens of Paul's day before examining the Athens of our own day.

3

PAUL'S ATHENS

In Paul's world, the word *Athens* brought to mind several things for most people, much like *Cambridge* or *Berkeley* might for people today. To understand better both the narrative in Acts and how it can be applied to our situation today, it is important to understand the general cultural and intellectual context of the actual Athens in first-century Greece and of the modern Athens in which we find ourselves. In this chapter, then, we will look briefly at the intellectual, cultural and historical status of ancient Athens and connect that to Paul's speech there. Then we will look in chapter four at the intellectual, cultural and historical-political situation in which we meet modern Athenians.

Acts 17 gives the impression that Paul did not originally have Athens on his list of places to go to and proclaim the gospel. He might well have stayed in Thessalonica for some time, perhaps a year or more, if he had not been essentially chased out of town by Jews with the aid of some local thugs for hire (Acts 17:5). This was not the first time, or the last, that some of the Jews who did not put faith in Jesus the Messiah responded to the missionaries out of jealousy that led to violence. Paul's regular practice in Macedonia as elsewhere was to follow major Roman roads (in this case, the Via Egnatia, a military road) and go to major cities to preach the gospel. This took him to Philippi, a Roman colony established to keep retired soldiers out of Rome, followed by Thessalonica, the provincial capital of Macedonia and a key center of the religious cult for the Roman emperors. The Christians in Thessalonica, "the brothers," sent Paul and

Silas by night to Berea, a town far off the Via Egnatia, and not likely to attract the persecutors from Thessalonica. (See figure 3.1.)

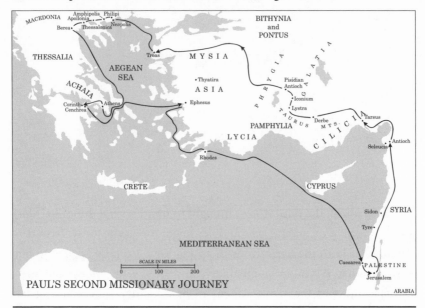

Figure 3.1. Paul's second missionary journey

This worked temporarily, but eventually the same agitators in Thessalonica showed up in Berea, and Paul once again had to leave town quickly for the sake of his own safety. The brothers took Paul to the sea and then on to Athens, where they left him to await the arrival of Silas and Timothy. We cannot be sure if Paul's original plans included traveling to Athens, but in Acts 17 it seems that he is taken there by other believers in order to escape persecution.

Athens the Great City

If you were putting together an itinerary of must-see cities in this region during Paul's time, Athens would be high on the list. Although the status and glory that Athens possessed in the fifth century B.C. when Plato taught there had diminished, it was still seen as a major center of intellectual and cultural achievement. Along with Alexandria in Egypt and Tarsus in Cilicia, Athens was one of the three greatest university cities in the known world. Athens boasted a long line of influential philosophers. In addition to Plato, there were Zeno, Epictetus, Epicurus and Aristotle (who made Athens his adopted home). The golden years of Athens, however, were back in the sixth through fourth centuries B.C., when tyrants were overthrown and replaced with democracy. From this period come historians such as Thucydides and Xenophon, the famous rhetorician Demosthenes, and the playwrights Menander and Aristophanes. By Paul's day, however, Athens was living on the memories of its glorious past.

Luke's comment in Acts 17:21 that both native Athenians and foreigners visiting Athens spent their time trying to learn of the latest (intellectual) ideas seems rather dismissive of these philosophers. Yet, Luke's statement expresses well the continuing attraction of Athens "as the city which more than any other evoked and preserved the greatness of Greek culture." Luke has also captured the sense of self-indulgence and faded glory that had probably characterized Athens for decades, if not centuries.[1] The poet Ovid referred to Athens as "learned Athens" (*Her.* 2.83). So, although Athens no longer wielded significant political power, it was still considered the place to go for Greek learning and culture, *the* place for the intellectual elite. In line with that, unlike major cities in the Greco-Roman world like Ephesus, Antioch in Syria, Rome or Corinth, Athens was not a major center of commerce. It seems to have been more like a backwater provincial city of only about twenty-five thousand people, focused more on debating ideas than on business opportunities.

RELIGION IN ATHENS

Athens was also well known for religious devotion. The city's name comes from the Greek goddess Athena. The famous Greek writer Aeschylus said of Athens that it is "dear to the gods" (*Eum.* 869). The Areopagus, a rocky hill in Athens, which was briefly described in chapter two, was named for Ares, the Greek god of war. According to Pausanius, a second-century A.D. writer who wrote a detailed *Description of Greece,* Ares was tried there on the charge of murdering Poseidon's son (*Descr.* 1.28.5). The Areopagus is also referred to as Mars Hill. This is because the Greek god Ares became identified with the Roman god of war, Mars. The Areopagus was also the name of a council or court that met at the Areopagus, though later may have met in the agora (the marketplace). Thus *Areopagus* can refer to the court or the hill. In order to avoid ambiguity, the word *Areopagus* will be primarily used for the council, while *Mars Hill* will be used to refer to the hill itself.

Located southeast of Mars Hill, the Acropolis in Athens was the site of many temples. The most noteworthy of these was the Parthenon, a temple built in honor of Athena, the city's patron deity. Next to the Parthenon was a circular temple dedicated to Roma and Augustus, which shows that Athens was involved in the imperial cult. Luke's comment that Paul's spirit was provoked within him when he saw that Athens was "full of idols" fits what we know of Athens at the time. A contemporary of Paul, the Roman satirist Petronius, has a character in the *Satyricon* state regarding Athens that "it is easier to meet a god in the street than a human" (*Sat.* 17). Although an altar to an unknown god has not been found, writers from this period attest to the existence of several of these. For example, in describing his trip from the harbor to Athens, Pausanias wrote of "altars of the 'Unknown gods'" (*Descr.* 1.1.4). Apollonius of Tyana spoke of Athens as the place where there are "altars of 'Unknown gods'" (Philostratus, *Vit. Apoll.* 6.3).[2]

Figure 3.2. The goddess Athena, for whom Athens was named. This statue is a Roman copy from the first or second century A.D. made from a fifth century B.C. original, known as the Athena Parthenos.

PHILOSOPHY IN ATHENS

While Athens was a very religious city, it was of course most well known as the center of Greek philosophy. This began perhaps with Socrates (c. 469–399 B.C.), who was executed for introducing strange gods to Athens, an event that would have been evoked by Luke's narrative of Paul announcing deities heretofore unknown in Athens and "certain astonishing things" (Acts 17:19-20). What we know of Socrates comes from Plato, who established the Academy in Athens around 385 B.C.

For the next nine centuries, philosophers and wannabe philosophers came to Athens to study at Plato's Academy. Much of Western thought through the centuries is built upon or indebted to Platonism, including certain aspects of the Western church's theology. (A couple of these Greek doctrines are the soul's inherent immortality—though the Bible, on the contrary, emphasizes the immortality of the physical resurrection body—and divine impassibility; that is, God cannot be affected or changed by any outside influence or agent.)[3] Aristotle, Plato's most famous student, studied here, and Aristotle would go on to instruct his most famous pupil, Alexander the Great.

The Epicureans, with whom Paul debated, were the intellectual descendants of Epicurus, who founded his own school of philosophy, called the Garden, in Athens in 307/6 B.C. We will look more at the specific views of the Epicureans and Stoics in chapter five when we look at Paul's audience. Here we will take only a brief look at these philosophies.

Platonism. In our day, when someone talks about "going to heaven," images of disembodied people sitting on clouds and playing harps often come to mind.[4] A Christian's soul, now freed from the prison of mortal flesh, exists forever in bliss. This view is often connected with the practice most seen of monks abusing their own bodies or at least denying their bodies (such as during Lent) in order to overcome the passions of their "evil flesh." You might be surprised to learn that these ideas and practices have their roots in the philosophy of Plato rather than the teachings of Paul. Plato was well known for his philosophical system. For him, all things visible here on earth, from people to plants to puppies to palaces, were inferior copies of the ideal person, plant, puppy or palace. As I type this, I am sitting in a chair, which exhibits some of the features of chairness, the essence of the ideal chair. By this concept, Plato meant that the ideal was better than the material things we can see, touch, taste, smell and hear. By Paul's day, the result of this thinking was not only to see humans, objects, plants and so forth as imperfect examples of the ideal for each of these, but to see them quite negatively. This was expressed in various religious and philosophical perspectives by asceticism, a rigorous physical abstinence or self-denial. This sprang from the view that the human body—a prison from which philosophers, following Plato, longed to escape—is a bad thing.

In the second century A.D. this became the view that the supreme god did not create the world, which is matter and therefore evil. Below this supreme god was a series of emanations, a chain of deities, with each deity being less powerful and perfect than the one above it. One of these demigods created the material world. This belief is known as Gnosticism. The god that made the world, therefore, was evil, and through learning secret knowledge (*gnōsis* in Greek), one learned how to escape the material world. This view was often combined with the Christian faith. One way this was done was by writing gospels, acts of some apostle or letters that claimed to be written by the apostles, such as the *Apocryphon of John*. The early church recognized these works to be forgeries, and today they are called pseudepigrapha, which has nothing to do with pigs. The word comes from two Greek words: *pseudos,* "false," and *graphē,* "a writing." One representation of this is in a pseudonymous gospel that claims that when Jesus walked on the earth, he left no footprints because if Jesus was divine, he certainly could not have had a physical body.[5] Most philosophical systems and ways of understanding reality, until recent centuries, were based on the views of Plato or of his student Aristotle, who developed his own philosophy and had a greater appreciation for the physical world and its workings.

Epicureanism. If we could bring an Epicurean from Paul's world to our twenty-first-century Western culture, that person would find much in common between Epicureanism and current trends and ideas that shape the lives of many people. If one watches television, it's not hard to notice the way that commercials appeal to the desire for pleasure and avoidance of pain. Buying the next version of a smartphone or a high-end car with more luxury features will make your life better, we are told. Nor can one miss the clear message from many directions that there is no higher good in life than sexual intercourse with whomever one wishes. Many universities have a reputation for being party schools, where the focus is on having fun, not on learning or forming a virtuous character (which was a significant concern in Paul's world). Especially with the growth of atheism or scientific naturalism among many, anything goes, because there is no life after death. In such views, humans are reduced to animated protoplasm—mere random arrangement of atoms—that one day will perish, and that is that. The caricature of Epicureanism certainly fits our culture well: "Let us eat, drink, and be merry for tomorrow we die."[6]

The philosopher Epicurus taught in Athens from about 306 to 290 B.C.

While Epicurus's school had many pupils, there were few who showed creativity in expanding or modifying his ideas. Therefore, the teaching of Epicurus continued to be taught in the Garden for centuries. Named for Epicurus, his teachings or philosophical system came to be called Epicureanism. The purpose of philosophy and the highest goal in life was pleasure, the "absence of pain in the body and trouble in the soul" (Diogenes Laertius, *Vit.* 10.131). The goal of Epicureanism was to live a happy life and maximize pleasure and friendship, which were the ideal values. This involved withdrawing from civic activities. Epicurus also taught the importance of forgoing immediate pleasures for more long-term pleasures in the future.

Figure 3.3. Bust of Epicurus, 270 B.C. Epicurus founded a school of philosophy called the Garden in Athens in 307/6 B.C.

The life of pleasure must be marked by wisdom and justice. The core concept for Epicurus was atomism. Everything, including the soul and the gods, was made of indivisible particles known as atoms, which were always in motion. Things were formed when atoms collided and stayed together. These collisions, however, were not uniform but random. Epicurus called the random movement of atoms the swerve, and he taught that the swerve means that everyone has free will. Furthermore, Epicurus taught that matter was eternal, uncreated and not endowed with any divine purpose.

Epicurus sought to remove the fear of death. He taught that the soul does not survive death but that the atoms of a person's soul disintegrate at death. There was no place in this system for bodily resurrection or even future spiritual existence. The Epicureans also taught that the gods, made of immortal matter, existed in a place of supreme pleasure but did not interfere in human affairs. This belief would release an adherent from both fear of the supernatural now and judgment in the afterlife. This provided the grounds for functional atheism: there may be gods or goddesses, but they are irrelevant to our existence, and therefore belief in their existence was of no significance. This is another similarity with modern culture. Many who believe vaguely in some sort of god do not live in light of that belief. Epicurus taught that moderation was important for happiness. His first followers avoided politics and ate simple fare. By Paul's day, however, Epicureanism was seen by many as the philosophy of living for (the pursuit of) pleasure with no higher goal in life, and hence was seen as less than virtuous.

Stoicism. Back in the 1990s one often saw T-shirts or bumper stickers that read, "Life is hard and then you die." While T-shirts did not exist over two millennia ago, such a shirt could have been worn by a Stoic. The Stoics, who were more influential than the Epicureans, had their own ideas about reality. Stoicism, introduced by Zeno, asserted that God was the divine Logos—or, Cosmic Reason. The Stoics were pantheists. They believed that everything was god and god was everything. Humans have a divine spark within themselves, and, at death, this spark returns to the divine reason. For Stoics, reason was the primary path to understanding god, as well as other areas of life. They would not have looked for evidence of the existence of the divine Logos because one discovered the Logos and its attributes through human reason, not through nature or other realities. Soon after Zeno's death, so-called Middle Stoicism emerged, which accommodated elements of Platonic and Aristotelian ideas. Later, well-known Stoics, such as Epictetus (see below) and Seneca, a contemporary of Paul (and tutor of Nero), presented Stoicism more as a way of life than as a system of philosophy.

In contrast to Epicureans, Stoics lived by an austere moral code. In Paul's day, the contemporary Stoic philosopher Epictetus (as recorded by Arrian) taught his students that it was worthless to study logic or cosmology for its own sake. Instead, it was crucial that they apply formal logic and cosmological premises to the improvement of their own moral will and life (Arrian, *Epict. diss.* 1.4.1-17). Epictetus taught that being calm and severe was the best course for humanity. Like other Stoics, Epictetus taught that the only good that people could do was to control their own moral choices. Absolutely everything else was outside of human control, and therefore, these things were morally indifferent. To desire things such as wealth or reputation was "irrational and the cause of all human misery." Happiness could be found only in the studied discernment of impulses to desire or avoid things and the rejection of these desires of anything under one's control.[7] Since the Stoics believed that everything, including their souls, was part of the Divine Logos (Divine Reason), when faced with suffering, their only answer was suicide. This was because there was no separate, personal god to appeal to for help. In fact, since the divine Reason was infused into everything, all events that occurred, including illness, natural disasters and war, were part of a goal-oriented rational process. Thus, all events were determined. This not only removed any sense of free will, but it also led to the denial of evil since all things were rationally worked out by the divine Logos.

Many people in the Roman Empire, of course, would have gotten a superficial understanding of these various philosophical perspectives through popular culture. Although they would not necessarily know the finer points, many would be familiar with the basic tenets of the Epicureans, Platonists, Stoics and other philosophical movements, even if they did not have the leisure to sit around debating the latest philosophical ideas.

SUMMARY

In Paul's day, Athens was well known for being the heart and soul of Greek philosophy, and this was the primary basis of Athens's prestige. Athens was also a very religious city, with temples and altars to traditional Greek gods and goddesses, foreign deities including Roman imperial deities, and even unknown gods. Athens's political power and status as a university town had declined by Paul's day, and with the city's focus on intellectual life, it never became an important center of commerce like neighboring cities. Thus, residents of and visitors to Athens would have found an intellectually stimulating environment, with many competing worldviews from which to choose.

4

OUR ATHENS

The cosmopolitan Paul was shaped by Jewish ethnicity and religion, by Roman citizenship, and by Greek culture—though he was ultimately rooted in yet another, more ultimate sphere: being "in the Messiah Jesus" (Rom 8:1).[1] As this book shows, Paul was superbly equipped to bring the good news to the Athenians. But what does our own Athens look like today? We must understand our own setting in order to communicate the good news of Jesus effectively and relevantly.

In Paul's day, we've noted, the three great centers of learning were Athens, Alexandria and his own Tarsus, and he spoke engagingly and insightfully with Stoics and Epicureans. Today, we in the West have our own schools of philosophy found in bastions of higher learning like Harvard and Berkeley, Oxford and Cambridge. Although we speak of "ivory towers" and the "hallowed halls of academia," many of the ideas bandied about within ivy-covered buildings have consequences, and the prevailing ideas in the academy eventually trickle down to popular culture to make an impact on how the average person on the street thinks and acts. Think of how Marxist ideas were taught in universities and expounded in academic books, but ultimately affected the lives of tens of millions of people through murder and oppression.[2]

Here is something else to consider. Although the Christian faith has profoundly influenced Western culture and although Christians have been at the forefront of preserving books and promoting education throughout church history, Western Christians are increasingly biblically illiterate and have no idea of what it means to "think Christianly." We live in a society in which we are "amusing ourselves to death," as Neil Postman once wrote.[3] We are so caught up with entertainment and technology that virtue and deep thought are gradually eclipsed. Church historian Mark Noll rightly laments this Christian anti-intellectualism in *The Scandal of the Evangelical Mind.* Many evangelical Christians have failed to appreciate the life of the mind for the glory of God.[4]

This is why studying Paul's speech in Athens serves as a model for Christians: we must be aware of the leading, influential ideas that shape culture so that we can insightfully and winsomely engage them with the power, beauty and truth of the gospel. Paul was not ignorant of those dominant ideas in his day, and we shouldn't be either. Paul also promoted robust, mature thinking—as opposed to being mentally infantile and doctrinally mushy (1 Cor 14:20; Eph 4:13; cf. Heb 5:14; 1 Pet 1:13).

As we point out in this book, many of the Greek philosophical ideas from Paul's day continue to impact our own culture. Yet not a few Christians are suspicious of philosophy and other academic disciplines as somehow opposed to God's grace and the working of God's Spirit. Embracing this anti-intellectual narrative may be why Christians have tended to view Paul's visit to Athens as a failure: "If Paul made a mistake in using philosophical and other cultural ideas to connect with the Athenians, then Christians should steer clear of them." If, however, Paul was actually making a wise use of philosophical and cultural resources to build bridges for the gospel, then we should pay close attention to how we can do this in our own day.

THE BENEFITS OF PHILOSOPHY AND OTHER CULTURAL RESOURCES

How frequently do we hear about well-meaning pastors who discourage young Christians from studying philosophy? For support, they will commonly cite Paul's warning against "empty philosophy" (Col 2:8) or his strong words about the "word of the cross" being "foolishness to those who are perishing" (1 Cor 1:18 NASB).

As it turns out, Paul was no stranger to philosophy. As we have seen, Stoicism had sprung up in Paul's home city of Tarsus—an intellectual center of his day that had surpassed even Athens.[5] Tarsus was the native city of the "second" Stoic Zeno. Other Stoic philosophers such as Antipater, Athenodorus (Cordylian) and Archedemus were born there. And the Stoic poet Aratus, whom Paul cited at Athens (Acts 17:28), was born near Tarsus in Soli. At Athens, Paul demonstrated his philosophical skills, revealing both the strengths and weaknesses of Stoicism and Epicureanism.[6]

Figure 4.1. A paved road in Tarsus from the second century B.C. Tarsus was one of three great centers of learning in the Roman Empire, along with Athens and Alexandria, Egypt.

Beyond this, Luke approvingly presents Paul as a philosopher who does the sorts of things that the early Greek philosopher Socrates does. Notice in table 4.1[7] the language being used of Paul in Acts 17 and its similarity to that of Plato's report of Socrates in his dialogue, *The Apology of Socrates*.

Table 4.1. Comparison of Paul's Language in Acts 17 and Plato's Report of Socrates in *The Apology of Socrates*

Paul	Socrates
Paul engaged in *dialogues* (*dielegeto*) in the *marketplace/agora* (*en tē agora*) "every day with those who happened to be present" (Acts 17:17).	Regarding *dialogues,* Socrates says, "I go about the world, obedient to the god, and search and make enquiry into the wisdom of any one, whether citizen or stranger" (*Apology* 23). Regarding the *marketplace,* he says, "If I defend myself in my accustomed manner, and you hear me using words which I have been in the habit of using in the *agora* . . ." (Plato, *Apol.* 17).
Paul is accused of proclaiming "foreign gods/ divinities [*zenōn daimoniōn*]" (Acts 17:18).	"Socrates is a doer of evil, who corrupts the youth; and who does not believe in the gods of the city, but has other new divinities [*hetera de daimonia kaina*]" (*Apol.* 24).
Paul is asked to give an account of his "new teaching [*kainē . . . didachē*]" (Acts 17:19).	"Socrates is a doer of evil, who corrupts the youth; and who does not believe in the gods of the city, but has other new [*kaina*] divinities" (*Apol.* 24).

As one scholar writes, "Luke indicates the favourable reception which the [Areopagus] address should receive from his hearers in the Greek world by this association of Paul with Socrates."[8] Paul used philosophical tools at his disposal, all the while setting his speech within a solidly biblical framework.

In a post-Christian age, to quote the Scriptures as an authoritative holy book in public settings can be counterproductive. The common reply is, "Well, I respect that you're a Bible-believer, but what about the Qur'an or the Book of Mormon?" To say "the Bible says" or "thus says the Lord" is appropriate in a Christian setting, but this approach will often fail to connect with outsiders to the church because they don't accept biblical authority.

But if we can't "just quote the Bible," where do we go? This isn't an attempt to diminish biblical authority, although we'll say more on this topic later. God has revealed himself specifically through Scripture and Jesus Christ, but he has revealed himself generally. He hasn't left himself "without witness" to those who have never picked up or even seen a Bible (Acts 14:17 NASB).

What we are urging is that we, like Paul, attempt to uphold biblical truths indirectly—through appealing to philosophical, scientific, historical and cultural insights that reinforce the gospel and a biblical outlook. After all, many in our culture consider the biblical message to be an irrelevant fairy tale—intellectually weak and perhaps even dangerous. Caricatures and false impressions prevent people from considering the Christian faith to be a viable, robust intellectual and spiritual alternative. The former atheist Holly Ordway tells of her experience as a nonbeliever:

> My problem could not be solved by hearing a preacher asserting that Jesus loved me and wanted to save me. I didn't believe in God to begin with, and I thought the Bible was a collection of folktales and myths, just like the stories I'd read of Zeus and Thor, Cinderella and Sleeping Beauty. Why should I bother to read the Bible, much less take seriously what it said about this Jesus? ... The problem lay deeper: in my very concept of what faith was. I thought faith was by definition irrational, that it meant believing some assertion to be true for no reason. It had never occurred to me that there could be a path to faith through reason, that there were arguments for the existence of God, and evidence for the claims of Christianity.[9]

What are some of these cultural bridges to help reinforce the Christian message?

PHILOSOPHICAL BRIDGES

If today's Athenians don't even think that God exists, then this will put the gospel further out of reach for them. That is, the gospel message presumes God's existence. And if people in our culture come to see that God's existence makes good sense—that it isn't at all the stuff of pure fairy tales or sheer fantasy—then they will more likely see the gospel as a more viable consideration.

You will be heartened to know that in our lifetime, philosophical journals and academic books have burst forth from the presses offering serious and sophisticated arguments for God's existence. In our generation, we have seen a powerful resurgence of Christian philosophy that serious-minded academics have to take seriously. So God has not left himself without a witness in the discipline of philosophy! The existence of a good, intelligent, powerful and personal God makes better sense of the fundamental features of the universe and human experience than do naturalism or Eastern philosophical alternatives. (See table 4.2.) In fact, many naturalists themselves acknowledge that their worldview lacks the robust resources to account for free will, objective moral values, rationality, consciousness, beauty, personhood and so on.[10]

"Facts are stubborn things," said John Adams at the Boston Massacre trial in December 1770. Just as Adams appealed to stubborn facts to defend innocent British soldiers who resisted an angry colonial mob, so we too should make use of stubborn facts pertaining to human beings embedded in the natural world. The image of God in humans—including personhood, consciousness, free will, spirituality and the longing for transcendence, deep relationality, moral responsibility and imagination—is one of those stubborn things that can't be eradicated by depersonalizing, reductionistic naturalism or Eastern worldviews.[11]

EARLY CHRISTIAN USE OF PHILOSOPHY

Perhaps here is a good place to note that early on church fathers saw the benefits of philosophy in understanding and promoting the Christian faith. We'll see later that the North African church father Tertullian (A.D. 160–225) was skeptical about what Athens (reason) had to do with Jerusalem (faith). While he himself argued for the truth of Christian faith over against what Athens taught, he also used the same forms of rhetorical arguments that the philosophers, and Paul himself, used before his day.

Table 4.2. Theism's Greater Explanatory Power over Naturalism

Phenomena We Observe, Assume or Recognize	Theistic View	Naturalistic View
(Self-) consciousness exists.	God is supremely *self-aware/conscious.*	The universe was produced by *mindless, nonconscious* processes.
Personal beings exist.	God is a *personal* Being.	The universe was produced by *impersonal* processes.
We believe we make free personal decisions/choices, assuming humans are accountable for their actions.	God is spirit and a free Being, who can *freely choose to act* (e.g., to create or not).	We have emerged by material, *deterministic* processes beyond our control.
Secondary qualities (colors, smells, sounds, tastes, textures) exist throughout the world.	God creates a world with many available *pleasurable and joyful* experiences.	The universe was produced by *mindless* material particles and deterministic processes.
We trust our senses and rational faculties as generally reliable in producing true beliefs.	A God of truth and *rationality* exists.	Because of our impulse to survive and reproduce, our beliefs would only help us *survive,* but a number of these could be completely *false.*
Human beings have intrinsic value/ dignity and rights.	God is the supremely *valuable* Being.	Human beings were produced by *valueless* processes.
Objective moral values exist.	God's character is the source of *goodness/moral values.*	The universe was produced by *nonmoral* processes.
The universe began to exist a finite time ago—without previously existing matter, energy, space or time.	A *powerful, previously existing* God brought the universe into being without any preexisting material. (Here, *something* emerges from *something.*)	The universe came into existence *from nothing by nothing*—or was, perhaps, self-caused. (Here, *something* comes from *nothing.*)
First life emerged.	God is a *living,* active Being.	Life somehow emerged from *nonliving* matter.
The universe is finely tuned for human life (known as "the Goldilocks effect"—the universe is "just right" for life).	God is a wise, *intelligent* Designer.	All the cosmic constants *just happened to be right;* given enough time and/or many possible worlds, a finely tuned world eventually emerged.
Beauty exists—not only in landscapes and sunsets but in "elegant" or "beautiful" scientific theories.	God is *creative.*	Beauty in the natural world is superabundant and in many cases *superfluous* (often not linked to survival).
We (tend to) believe that life has purpose and meaning. For most of us, life is worth living.	God has created/designed us for certain *purposes* (to love him and others, etc.); when we live them out, our lives find meaning/enrichment.	There is *no cosmic purpose,* blueprint or goal for human existence.
Real evils—both moral and natural—exist/take place in the world.	Evil's definition assumes a design plan (how things *ought* to be, but are not) or standard of goodness (a corruption or absence of goodness) by which we judge something to be evil. God is a good Designer; his existence supplies the crucial moral context to make sense of evil.	Atrocities, pain and suffering just happen. This is just how things *are*—with no ultimate "plan" or standard of goodness to which things *ought* to conform.

Unquestionably, the early church fathers were drawn to the writings of Plato and Aristotle. As seen in the Platonic dialogues, philosophy, which was well established long before Paul went to Athens, taught that bad arguments should be exposed, that there should be intolerance for sloppy thinking and that it was important to search for good arguments. The search for truth was essential. Some Christians rejected philosophy completely as being "the wisdom of the world" that Paul allegedly rejected in 1 Corinthians 1–2; this is a terribly misunderstood text, as we have seen. Many other Christians, however, were comfortable with the wisdom of the philosophers and accepted their premises.

Figure 4.2. Head of Socrates, Roman copy of a Greek original, fourth century B.C. Since Socrates (c. 469–399 B.C.) left no writings, all that we know of him comes from the writings of his student, Plato.

Perhaps the best example of this was Justin Martyr (ca. A.D. 100–167). Justin was perhaps the greatest of the apologists, those early Christians who wrote works to show the superiority of Christian beliefs over those of the philosophers. Trained with a classical education, he was drawn to the style of Socrates and was a dedicated follower of Plato's philosophy.

Justin became a believer in Christ during the time of Roman persecution against Christians. He was initially impressed by the courage and hope of Christians in the face of death. The chief influence in his becoming a believer, however, was his encounter with a mysterious man by the sea. This man told Justin of the prophets who foretold the coming of the Messiah, and he warned Justin against following empty philosophy without being a lover of deeds and truth. Justin came to realize that the Christian faith was the "true philosophy," and he believed that Plato's philosophy actually cut off flesh-and-blood humans from realizing the perfect world, a gap that was bridged by Jesus, the Word made flesh.

Justin wrote that common sense dictates that we should only hold true beliefs and reject false beliefs of those who preceded us. Justin shared with the philosophers a commitment to the preeminence of truth and the dignity of the quest to find it. He demonstrated this by traveling to Rome, where he set up a school specifically to teach Christians how to dialogue with the culture in a way that could be understood by those trained in classical philosophy. In this way the elaborate methods of philosophy were incorporated into Christian culture as a way to challenge culture. This led to philosophical concepts being harnessed for Christian needs.[12]

Another church father who utilized philosophy in the face of anti-intellectualism and heresy was Augustine (A.D. 354–430).[13] Augustine grew up in North Africa, where the Christianity he encountered was superstitious and opposed to honest questioning and to the life of reason. Two North African church fathers exerted a strong—but, unfortunately, anti-intellectual—influence there. Both were bishops in Carthage (in modern-day Tunisia). The first was Tertullian, who, as we noted, thought philosophy and faith had nothing to do with each other. Then there was Cyprian (A.D. 200–258), who was only slightly less strident than his predecessor. Both of them believed God had a body and that only the physical is real.

During the following century, Augustine was left troubled by these theological and philosophical confusions. He thought long and hard about two vexing problems. The first had to do with the origin of evil. The second had to do with the nature of God: If God is physical, he wondered, does he have hair and a beard? And if God is physical, he must be diffused throughout infinite space so that there is more of God in an elephant than in a sparrow.

Around the age of eighteen, Augustine read the first-century B.C. Roman orator and philosopher Cicero's *Hortensius,* a philosophical work that inspired Augustine in the love and pursuit of wisdom. Because Augustine assumed the Christian faith was intrinsically anti-intellectual, he joined up with the Manichees, who said that good and evil are eternally opposed principles.

Through the influence of the philosophical mind of Ambrose of Milan (ca. A.D. 340–397), Augustine saw the value of Neo-Platonic philosophy to help answer these two burning questions—answers that would help lead to his conversion in A.D. 386. How did Ambrose help Augustine to see with greater philosophical clarity that, as he put it, led him to a "new land"?

Regarding evil, Augustine realized that evil is not a substance or a thing in itself. Evil is a corruption or distortion of what is good, like a pothole in a road or a falcon without wings. *Being* is good since a good God made all things "very good." Evil is a corruption of what is good. We can't understand crookedness without an understanding of straightness, nor can we make sense of counterfeit money without an understanding of authentic currency. In the same way, evil can't exist without goodness since evil is parasitic on the good.

As for Augustine's understanding of God, he came to reject divine corporeality (that God has a body or is physical). He realized that God, like the soul, is a spiritual substance. God is not physical, nor does he take up infinite space. Augustine realized that his own ideas were indeed real, but they didn't take up any space. Even though Augustine as a Christian theologian would reject aspects of Neo-Platonic philosophy—for example, that all things emanate or flow from the impersonal One—he was indebted to many of Neo-Platonism's insights to help resolve key philosophical stumbling blocks in his mind.

Augustine saw how the Christian faith expanded the mind, stating, *Credo ut intelligam*, that is, "I believe that I may understand." A question was raised by the heretical Manichees: "What did God do before he made heaven and earth?" Being a truth seeker, Augustine disliked the mocking answer that unthinking North African Christians shot back: "He was preparing hell . . . for those prying into such deep subjects." Augustine wanted to take such questions seriously, and he refused to evade "by a joke the force of the objection":

> It is one thing to see the objection; it is another to make a joke of it. I do not answer in this way. I would rather respond, "I do not know," concerning what I do not know rather than say something for which a man inquiring about such profound matters is laughed at while the one giving a false answer is praised.[14]

Augustine was also quite insightful when it came to Christianity and science. Chiding fellow Christians for making rather embarrassing and misguided remarks about matters scientific, Augustine wrote:

> It is a disgraceful and dangerous thing for an infidel to hear a Christian, presumably giving the meaning of Holy Scripture, talking nonsense on these topics; and we should take all means to prevent such an embarrassing situation, in which people show up vast ignorance in a Christian and laugh it to scorn. . . . If they find a Christian mistaken in a field which they themselves

know well and hear him maintaining his foolish opinions about our books, how are they going to believe those books in matters concerning the resurrection of the dead, the hope of eternal life, and the kingdom of heaven, when they think their pages are full of falsehoods on facts which they themselves have learnt from experience and the light of reason?[15]

Like the apostle Paul, Augustine was a master of rhetorical skills, and, also like Paul, he used these skills to persuade people to love the way of wisdom—the way of truth, goodness and beauty as revealed in the triune God:

Late have I loved you, O beauty ever ancient, ever new. Late have I loved you. You have called to me, and have called out, and have shattered my deafness. You have blazed forth with light and have put my blindness to flight! You have sent forth fragrance, and I have drawn in my breath, and I pant after you. I have tasted you, and I hunger and thirst after you. You have touched me, and I have burned for your peace.[16]

As this quotation reveals, Augustine clearly loved God deeply while at the same time being a brilliant thinker who used his gifts for God's glory. A little reflection reveals just how impoverished we Christians would be without such thoughtful giants throughout church history—from the apostle Paul to Justin Martyr, Augustine, Irenaeus, Anselm and Thomas Aquinas to the modern era's gifted thinkers such as Jonathan Edwards, C. S. Lewis, Alvin Plantinga and William Lane Craig. Over the centuries, many Christian theologians and philosophers have courageously defended the Christian faith against false teachings and pernicious

Figure 4.3. While Augustine lived from A.D. 354 to 430, this painting of him by Antonello da Messina was done in 1472–1473. Augustine was perhaps the greatest theologian of the early church.

heresies, and without them the church would be severely weakened theologically as well as intellectually marginalized. C. S. Lewis said that we need good philosophy, if for no other reason than that bad philosophy should be answered.

Many Christians who sit in the pews on Sunday mornings denigrate the life of the mind. "Don't give me theology and philosophy. Just give me Jesus," they may say. "It's all a matter of the heart." But why not both—being Spirit-filled and Spirit-empowered Christians of heart and mind? Scripture itself demands greater thoughtfulness of us as stewards of God's good gift of the intellect. Intellectual laziness or anti-intellectualism is a sin. That doesn't mean that strengthening our minds, like our characters, is easy. The mind is very much like a muscle, and the more we exercise this God-given capacity, the better we become at using it—and the more doors God can open for us as thinking Christians. Being thoughtful believers is a proper response to God's grace. As the hymn writer Frances Ridley Havergal wrote in "Take My Life,"

> Take my intellect and use
> ev'ry pow'r as Thou shalt choose.

As God's image bearers, we must not neglect to love the Lord with all our mind, which reflects God's own nature as all-knowing and all-wise. We must not be infants in our thinking (1 Cor 14:20). We should recognize that God can be glorified in the use of the mind. This doesn't mean that all Christians must be intellectuals or scholars, but they should all be thoughtful and reflect deeply about their faith, the world and how to communicate their faith to unbelievers.

SCIENTIFIC BRIDGES

In the twentieth century, scientists discovered that the universe of physical time, matter, energy and space came into existence a finite time ago. The Big Bang, astronomer Fred Hoyle labeled it: the universe is expanding; its energy is dissipating or spreading out (the second law of thermodynamics); and that static noise on our radios and TVs is a constant signal throughout space and is the aftereffect of the Big Bang itself (cosmic microwave background radiation). Scientists also saw that the universe is astonishingly finely tuned for life—what astrophysicists have called the Goldilocks effect: Earth is placed where it's not too hot or too cold, but just right. In addition, we live in an era when even naturalistic scientists are baffled by how consciousness could emerge from nonconscious matter. And try as they might to escape the notion of design, naturalists continually use design talk throughout their writings—cells being like factories, brains like computers, the human eye like the camera. In fact, Stanford University philosopher of science Timothy Lenoir, not a believer, confesses: "Teleological [design] thinking has been steadfastly resisted by modern biology. And yet, in nearly every area of research biologists are hard pressed to find language that does not impute purposiveness to living forms."[17]

Figure 4.4. Fred Hoyle (1915–2001) was a brash and brilliant astronomer who opposed the idea of an initial massive explosion as the explanation for the expanding universe. He derisively labeled the notion the "big bang," a name that stuck.

Many naturalistic scientists accuse theists of believing in the "God of the gaps": that God plugs the holes of our ignorance—until science comes along and fills them in with natural explanations of how things "really" work in the world. Yet the more we discover about the amazing world we inhabit, the more unlikely and unnatural these naturalistic explanations appear.

HISTORICAL BRIDGES

History is another discipline that assists us in our witness. As informed Christians know, remarkable historical support exists for the bodily resurrection of Jesus as an event of history. Four key historical facts are accepted by the majority of historians—and note, many of them don't treat the New Testament as a holy book but nevertheless recognize that it does offer solid, valuable historical information. These facts are: (1) Jesus' crucifixion under Pontius Pilate followed by his burial in Joseph of Arimathea's tomb; (2) the empty tomb, which was recognized by friend and foe alike; (3) the post-mortem appearances to the disciples (whether or not these were hallucinations not being an issue at this point); and (4) the sudden emergence of the early church, proclaiming the risen Christ in the heart of Jerusalem. And we could add the conversions of Jesus' brother James and Paul.[18] The historian N. T. Wright concludes that the combined historical probability of the empty tomb—something Jesus' enemies assumed (Mt 28:12-15)—and the post-mortem appearances is "virtually certain," being on the level of Caesar Augustus's death in A.D. 14 or the fall of Jerusalem in A.D. 70.[19]

Christians can appeal to other historical facts that bear out the living reality of the gospel. Consider its impact in Western civilization when it comes to the rise of modern science and the emphasis on human rights. As sociologist Rodney Stark notes, these "rested entirely on religious foundations, and the people who brought it about were devout Christians."[20] Physicist Paul Davies (not a Christian) noted: "Science began as an outgrowth of theology, and all scientists, whether atheists or theists . . . accept an essentially theological worldview."[21] And the famed scientist Robert Oppenheimer attributes the growth of modern science to the Christian faith.[22]

The fact of the biblical faith giving shape to the Western worldview that emphasizes human equality and rights is affirmed by leading atheist intellectuals as well. Atheist professor Jürgen Habermas is one of Europe's most prominent philosophers. He acknowledges the inescapable historical link between human rights discourse today and the biblical worldview:

> Christianity has functioned for the normative self-understanding of modernity as more than just a precursor or a catalyst. Egalitarian universalism, from which sprang the ideas of freedom and a social solidarity, of an autonomous conduct of life and emancipation, the individual morality of conscience, human rights, and democracy, is the direct heir to the Judaic ethic of justice and the Christian ethic of love. This legacy, substantially unchanged, has been the object of continual critical appropriation and reinterpretation. To this day, there is no alternative to it. And in light of current challenges of a postnational constellation, we continue to draw on the substance of this heritage. Everything else is just idle postmodern talk.[23]

Likewise, the late postmodern thinker Jacques Derrida, another atheist, made a similarly bold affirmation of the influence of the biblical faith in this regard:

> Today the cornerstone of international law is the sacred, what is sacred in humanity. You should not kill. You should not be responsible for a crime against this sacredness, the sacredness of man as your neighbor . . . made by God or by God made man. . . . In that sense, the concept of crime against humanity is a Christian concept and I think there would be no such thing in the law today without the Christian heritage, the Abrahamic heritage, the biblical heritage.[24]

We could appeal to other tools that reinforce the Christian worldview. Take, for example, the study of neuroscience and near-death experiences. Neuroscience reveals more and more how human beings are personal agents, selves with wills, who can actually reshape their brains by making choices and establishing new patterns, including the alteration of obsessive-compulsive disorders.[25] Documented near-death experiences and out-of-body experiences indicate that humans are more than mere material beings.[26] And rather than simply saying "the Bible says," we can appeal to sociological and psychological studies that reveal, say, the harmful psychological effects of abortion on women or the many problems brought on by cohabitation as opposed to marital commitment without first living together.[27] The list goes on.

ENGAGING SOME OF THE INFLUENTIAL IDEAS OF OUR DAY

Paul astutely addressed two schools of philosophical thought at Mars Hill, the Epicureans and the Stoics. Likewise, we too should be prepared to engage with several schools of thought that dominate our cultural landscape today.

Two coexisting, yet quite opposed, worldviews are very pronounced on university campuses today, and they find their expression in a bewildering assortment of perspectives. One we could call anti-realistic—dependent on human minds or the result of cultural/social constructions—and the other claims to be realistic and objective, though based on a narrow understanding of what the real world is.

Christian theism has had a long history and a pervasive influence in the West, and for many centuries this outlook held sway and largely became the fabric of our cultural tapestry. More recently, biblical theism has faced worldview competitors such as postmodernism and relativism (with certain spinoffs such as emotivism and pluralism), on the one hand, and naturalism and scientism, on the other. Let's look at these expressions of anti-realism more closely.

Postmodernism and relativism. Since the 1960s, we have lived in an era of truth decay. We commonly hear slogans such as "that's true for you but not for me" and "that's just your perspective." These are expressions of relativism—that truth isn't for all people but depends on one's perspective or circumstances. Relativists commonly label Christians as intolerant or judgmental for the simple fact that they believe Jesus is the only way of salvation or that they aren't open-minded about other alternatives, as though relativists are even remotely open to absolutes!

In light of the modernist era of failed metanarratives (or grand stories), like Communism and Nazism, that ravaged and destroyed millions in the twentieth century, postmodern thinking challenged the legitimacy of any story or worldview claiming to be true for every person (a metanarrative). After all, if you believe in some universal truths, then you'll end up oppressing those who disagree with you.

Prior to postmodernism, Westerners generally believed that truth did not depend on human constructions or subjective feelings. They recognized that truth, by definition, excluded something, namely, falsehood. Like a mirror, truth was thought to reflect reality, the way things really are. If a belief or story did not match up with reality—say, that the moon is made of cheese or that the earth is flat—then it was understood to be false. Truth has to do with faithfulness to reality; reality makes a belief true or false. My belief doesn't make reality true. One philosopher said that truth is like betting on a race horse: "The success or failure of our bet depends on whether the horse wins or not. That is, this is independent of us."[28] Only the world of what is—or more specifically, reality—confers truth or falsity.[29] Reality is the truth maker. This is a view known as realism.

For the postmodern, truth is a social construction, what can be called anti-realism. The social constructionist says that reality is whatever we make of it or however we perceive it. As Friedrich Nietzsche (1844–1900) said back in the nineteenth century, truth is a mobile army of metaphors, and those in power can manipulate language in an attempt to shape reality in the minds of people. It's like what postmodern thinker Richard Rorty has said: truth is what your peers let you get away with saying.[30]

Figure 4.5. Friedrich Wilhelm Nietzsche (1844–1900) was a highly influential philosopher who laid the foundation for much postmodern thought.

A large, though unwitting, influence in the direction of anti-realism was the philosopher Immanuel Kant (1724–1804). He said that our minds act as filters or lenses to interpret the world; he emphasized that we don't have access to the way things really are—only to the way things appear to us. Whereas the standard view used to be that truth and morality are discovered (realism), the postmodern emphasizes that they are invented or constructed by humans (anti-realism).

While there's a lot wrong with postmodernism, it emphasizes some important things: that we do see in a mirror dimly (1 Cor 13:12), that we have biases and limitations, and that we regularly have to deal with less than 100 percent certainty. Yet to follow the postmodern path beyond this point leads to all kinds of logical cul-de-sacs and moral pitfalls. For one thing, metanarratives—large explanatory systems or worldviews that claim to be true for all people—don't necessarily oppress. In fact, repudiating metanarratives or treating them with suspicion will lead to moral cowardice and the shriveling of our character. The problem with postmodernism's timidity about making truth claims is that it cannot condemn the very horrors of Nazi concentration camps and Soviet prisons that gave rise to postmodernism in the first place. Or at least it must stand by in moral helplessness to observe. The problem with German bystanders who could have protected Jews but didn't was not that they had strong moral convictions but that they lacked them! It was their moral indecisiveness or a lack of courage that we find blameworthy.

To many, postmodernism appears to offer an escape from moral and intellectual commitment. Yet to hold to the postmodernist denial or suspicion of universal truths and moral facts leads to intellectual and ethical bankruptcy. For example, those claiming that "there is no way things *really* are" are telling us the way things really are! And those saying we have no immediate access to reality presumably do have immediate access to reality to know at least this! And would we trust someone as a friend or a spouse who questions whether promise-keeping is a duty?

If we all have our own perspective and nothing more, then whose (rather authoritative) perspective is that? If there are no facts but only interpretations, as Nietzsche said, is that a fact or merely an interpretation? To claim that truth is relative or contextual is to make a statement that is not relative or contextual; it is absolute and objective—true for all, not just true for the relativist. Knowledge and truth are inescapable. To deny that we can know is to affirm that we can know—"I know that you can't know." To deny truth is to affirm that it's true that there is no truth. Even the most skeptical person takes for granted that his mental faculties are functioning properly. Even if he doubts everything, he believes he is thinking logically in doing so.

Even those claiming to be moral relativists are adopting a moral stance, one that they take to be true and applicable to all cultures and individuals. They will use logical arguments to defend the position that those believing in objective moral values are in error. Furthermore, relativists will not only typically give you nonrelative reasons for their viewpoint—for example, citing the undeniable fact that different people believe different things. They will also be selective about how they apply their relativism: they won't talk true-for-you language when it comes to sports scores, stock numbers, the capitals of states and countries, the latest traffic report, or the ingredients on labels at the drug store or supermarket. Rather, they will typically be relativists when it comes to religion and morality, the areas that allegedly interfere with their personal freedom.

At a personal level, the relativist fails to distinguish between persons and the beliefs they hold. Before relativism became so embedded in our culture, people could disagree agreeably. They could hold conflicting views yet show respect and civility toward each other as persons. As we point out later, cultivating relationships with relativists and building trust are important steps to countering the corrosive, soul-destroying worldview of relativism and postmodernism. As you connect with relativists, you'll often see a connection between their outlook and a background that lacks trusting personal relationships. And this presents an excellent opportunity for Christians to build these relational bridges with them.

Emotivism. In the worldview neighborhood, emotivism is just around the corner from relativism. This philosophy of life is centered on feelings or emotions, entirely or partially eclipsing truth from consideration. In ethics, emotivism stresses that statements like "Murder is wrong" don't express moral truths; they only express feelings: "I don't like murder" or "Murder—yuck!" With its emphasis on feelings, the Romantic movement in art, literature and philosophy begun in the early 1800s was a partial response to the seemingly cold, sterile rationalism of the Enlightenment (1650–1800). And in our day, we are witnessing something of a bright afterglow of Romanticism and the widespread flight from reason.

We encounter emotivism in the moral claim "I feel that this is right" or "That makes me feel uncomfortable." In their research papers, university students with increasing frequency write "I feel" rather than "I think" to establish their points. Some might ask, "Well, what's the difference? Aren't a person's feelings and opinions (thinking) pretty much the same thing?" No, they are not, and we should try to speak with greater precision—beyond the mere expression of feelings—with a view to actually reflecting on and assessing the truth content of beliefs.[31]

First of all, to say "I think" sounds more argumentative than "I feel." Also, our culture increasingly takes feelings to be self-justifying, as though no further argument or supporting reasons are necessary. And how can you disagree with how someone feels? Think of the person who says, "I like chocolate ice cream." That statement reflects a personal preference, someone's inner state, and there's no point in disagreeing with it. But what are we to do with it? It sounds authoritative, but are we to adopt chocolate ice cream as our own favorite?

Emotivism doesn't express moral facts, only moral preferences. The problem, though, is that feelings are often misguided, and we need good thinking to direct our emotions and help bring them under control. A person may get angry in a particular situation he has misjudged, but his anger may quickly subside when he hears reasons that explain the context. And don't we periodically change our moral perspective on certain issues, presumably because we think we have a good reason for doing so? But why should we take a person's feelings, by themselves, as authoritative?

Now we do have certain basic moral intuitions that are anchored in a God-given conscience that we should never ignore, something C. S. Lewis points out in the appendix to his *Abolition of Man*. Even though the conscience isn't infallible and needs refining, we can get a lot right by paying attention to our conscience and not stifling it. If our conscience is functioning even half decently, we can have a good start on recognizing basic moral truths—the wrongness of torturing babies for fun or mocking the mentally retarded. But when we get into moral discussions about, say, politics, the death penalty, or pacifism versus just war, only moral feelings seem to matter, without reasons or evidence to support such feelings. To say "I feel" says nothing about the rightness or wrongness of a particular war or the death penalty. By contrast, to say "I think" reflects rationality and intellectual content that can be discussed and debated. When we say, "I think," we imply reasons for our beliefs. "I feel" does not.

To reinforce the "I feel" over the "I think" message, movies, the Internet and other forms of entertainment diminish our capacity to think hard and to be disciplined in our reasoning. The pursuit of entertainment leads to a trivialization of culture. The late Neil Postman pointed out in *Amusing Ourselves to Death* that, unlike the printed word, the flitting images on the screen keep the eye moving, minimal comprehension skills are necessary, and the overarching goal is emotional gratification. The viewer is inundated with messages that he assimilates rather than logically processes. No prior knowledge is required for watching movies. And serious reasoning is not demanded, perplexity is not introduced, and elaborate reasoning is not permitted. If any intellectual demands happen to be placed on the viewer, he will just click the remote control to watch something else.[32]

So it is easy for the uncritical TV or movie watcher to assimilate cultural messages without thinking about them—the excitement about an illicit sexual relationship, the right to get out of a boring marriage, the rationalizing of cutting moral corners since "it's not hurting anyone." No wonder people imagine they can simply feel strongly about their beliefs without offering supporting arguments! René Descartes's familiar dictum "I think; therefore I am" has been replaced by the mantra "I feel; therefore I am."

Given the instability and unreliability of emotions, believers should all the more carve out a place for serious thinking about life and cultivate habits of the mind to do so. Rather than letting our culture press us into its mold, we are to reflect on what is our "reasonable [*logikos*] service" of worship in light of God's mercies (Rom 12:1-2 NET).[33] True disciples of Christ are to be characterized by "discernment," "wisdom" and "understanding" (Phil 1:9; Col 1:9). We are to discipline our minds to take proper action (1 Pet 1:13), to think Christianly about our faith and how to live out kingdom-centered priorities.

Emotivism can also take the form of anchoring authenticity in feelings. If a person doesn't feel like doing something, it's hypocritical to go against his feelings. And why teach children to apologize when they don't feel like saying they're sorry? Of course, the faulty assumption here is that our emotions are the sum total of who we are. This ignores other features of who we are—our will, our identity, our character and its formation, and our relationships and the promises we make to cultivate and nourish them. Our emotions are a small part of who we are, and to become robust human beings, we will deprive ourselves of what may feel good in the moment, that is, postponing gratification, in order to achieve something of greater worth. Seeking our own well-being over against loving God and others will ultimately put true life out of reach (Jn 12:25). When, by God's grace, we cultivate habits of obedience and self-denial, we are being intentional about the process of character formation so that doing the right thing, what we were designed for, becomes more and more second nature to us. We train children to cultivate the habit of apologizing after wronging others and expressing thanks for kindnesses shown because it is the right thing to do—even if they don't feel like doing so. Teaching them these habits is a reminder that their lives should not be driven by the whims of what they feel like doing. Rather, their lives are to be shaped by concerns for moral and spiritual formation to achieve the goal of our humanity, namely, Christlikeness.

In our therapeutic age, Westerners commonly view God as a divine therapist rather than as the cosmic authority who commands our obedience and allegiance. To those who trust in him, God gives the Holy Spirit, not the Happy Spirit. God is more interested in our being good and doing good than our feeling good; he is more interested in character transformation than self-authentication. God is not only concerned about sincerity, but also that sincere hearts be aligned with the truth; after all, people can be sincerely wrong, as history amply illustrates.

Only by losing our lives for Christ's sake, by taking up our cross daily, will we actually find what is life indeed (Mt 16:25; Jn 10:10). As we focus on right thinking and the importance of character formation, we will avoid the pitfalls of emotivism and maintain an appropriate critical distance from our culture's messages and morals (Rom 12:1-2). After all, often what is esteemed by our culture is detestable in God's sight (Lk 16:15).

Religious pluralism and syncretism. The TV show host Oprah Winfrey denied that there could be only one way to God. There are "millions of ways," she claimed.[34] This reflects a commonly held view that belief in one path to salvation is narrow-minded and arrogant. Religious pluralism maintains that there are many different paths to salvation or spiritual liberation, not just one. And on top of that, it's arrogant to say that Jesus is the only way of salvation (Jn 14:6; Acts 4:12). Sophisticated religious pluralists like the late John Hick do admit that genuine and significant, irreconcilable differences exist in the world's religions. For example, Buddhism's Dalai Lama acknowledges: "Among spiritual faiths, there are many different philosophies, some just opposite to each other on certain points. Buddhists do not accept a creator; Christians base their philosophy on that theory."[35] Buddhists, Hindus, Muslims and Christians will diverge on the nature of the human problem, the solution to the human problem, the afterlife and a host of other aspects to their religion. If there's one thing that the world's religions have in common, it's that they're so dramatically different from one another!

However, religious pluralism also maintains that religious beliefs are the result of cultural conditioning, and these religions are all doing the same thing—attempting to get at the ultimate reality (e.g., God, Brahman). And the pluralist believes that the world's religions, not just one, are equally capable of bringing salvation or liberation. How is this liberation realized? It comes through the move away from self-centeredness to reality-centeredness. The realization of this salvation is evidenced by the producing of saints, morally upright people, in the various religions, people such as Jesus, Mahatma Gandhi, and the Dalai Lama.[36]

Religious syncretism, on the other hand, blends differing—indeed, conflicting—religious beliefs into a unique system of thought and practice. This is apparent not only in certain versions of voodou (popularly rendered *voodoo*) in Haiti and New Orleans, as well as Santeria in Cuba, that incorporate Catholic saints and liturgy with pagan beliefs. Syncretism is also quite popular among those who prefer spirituality to religion. Many today will claim that they aren't religious but that they are spiritual. That is, they aren't "into" the publicly practiced and historically established rituals, creeds and dogmas of organized religion. Rather, they subscribe to a private, often undefined and vague mystical set of beliefs directed toward personal fulfillment, and these beliefs are typically cobbled together according to one's own preferences—a very Platonic, or more specifically Gnostic, way of thinking.

More and more Westerners prefer a buffet-line approach to spirituality: we pick and choose the religious views and practices that we like and reject whatever we don't. In our democratic, egalitarian, anti-elitist way of thinking, religion has come to be a matter of preference rather than truth. Back in 2002, the Barna Group polled Americans, even many professing Christians, and found that they are syncretistic about their religious beliefs. They will pick and choose beliefs from Islam, Wicca or Eastern religions.[37] A later survey reveals that only one out of ten professing Christians in America holds to a truly biblical worldview, as American Christianity reveals a high degree of biblical illiteracy. Being so poorly informed makes many professing Christians susceptible to syncretism.

How is the Christian to respond to syncretism and pluralism? We'll respond primarily to religious pluralism, but let's say a few things about syncretism. Syncretism in our Western culture tends to be a hodgepodge of beliefs assimilated through Internet surfing, movie watching, an intro to philosophy class in college and the most recent blog posts a person has read.

Many problems with syncretism are addressed earlier in the chapter in the discussion of postmodernism and relativism. Syncretism adopts conflicting beliefs without considering the relevance of logical laws or the background assumptions behind those adopted beliefs. One of us spoke recently with an atheist who nevertheless claimed she believes in miracles, which, in fact, presuppose the supernatural realm: a miracle is an event that would not have occurred if left up to natural processes. We have also encountered professing Christians who have so imbibed the waters of postmodernism that they tepidly claim we really can't know—despite the fact that they seem to know this. And as we look at Scripture itself, we see plenty of confident knowledge claims being made (e.g., Jn 17:3; Eph 3:19; 1 Jn 2:21; 5:13). And we should not forget that many Christians throughout history have been persecuted and martyred because of their confident assertions that they have truly known God in Christ.

The issue of syncretism raises a very relevant issue related to having a worldview or philosophy of life at all. A worldview is important in that it can help unify life and give it coherence. But this runs contrary to syncretism. One Christian apologist was once challenged by a young woman when he said that human beings look for coherence. "Where did you get this idea of coherence?" she asked. The gentleman replied, "Do you want a coherent answer, or will an incoherent one do?"[38] We find it difficult to live with obvious self-contradictions in our lives, and forming a worldview, whether we are conscious of it or not, is an attempt to bring such coherence to unify life and to guide our thinking and action.

One helpful definition of a worldview is that it is "an articulation of the basic beliefs embedded in a shared grand story that are rooted in a faith commitment and that give shape and direction to the whole of our individual and corporate lives."[39] Of course, the Christian metanarrative (grand story) is the drama of the eternal triune God who creates and, though his creatures turn away from him, brings about redemption leading to a renewed creation through Christ.

Now, a worldview or philosophy of life will make assumptions about key questions:

- Reality (metaphysics): What is real? Why does anything exist at all? Does God exist?

- Origins: Where have we come from?

- Human nature: Who are we? Do we have rights and value or not? What is the nature of our condition? What is the solution to our problem?

- Destiny: What is the nature of the afterlife? What happens at death?

- Knowledge: How do we know? Why believe anything at all?

- Ethics: Do objective moral values exist? How do we discern right from wrong?

- History: Does history have a purpose or goal? Is there any meaning to life?

Sometimes it is helpful to graciously ask the syncretist about the answers to these questions, and often this conversation will expose inconsistencies of thought and much ad hoc, patchwork reasoning. Yet in doing so, we must remember that a worldview is more than an intellectual belief system or grid for interpreting our experience. A worldview involves a heart commitment or orientation toward God or away from him. Syncretism—like other false belief systems—may simply be an attempt to pick and choose from the metaphysical buffet line to create reality according to one's own preferences.

Besides the personal commitment part, we must remember that worldviews are often subconscious, like a building's foundation or the skeleton of the body, and individuals may not even think about their assumptions or where they got their ideas. One philosopher, Alfred North Whitehead, offered this piece of advice:

> When you are criticizing the philosophy of an epoch, do not chiefly direct your attention to those intellectual positions which its exponents feel it necessary to defend. There will be some fundamental assumptions which adherents of all the variant systems within each epoch unconsciously presuppose. Such assumptions appear so obvious that people do not know what they are assuming because no other way of putting things has ever occurred to them.[40]

At the end of this book is a list of resources to assist you in conversations with unbelievers, including syncretists, and we would encourage you to spend time digesting the content of these books to better equip yourselves for this task.

What of religious pluralism? Though it claims that the world's religions are culturally conditioned, that would make this view itself culturally conditioned and, for that reason, no more superior or worthy of belief than, say, Buddhism or Christianity. If we simply grow up believing what we do because of where we're born, then what if you are born into a culture of religious pluralists? And what if we have good reasons for embracing the Christian faith and rejecting the dubious claims of pluralism?

Even though religious pluralism insists that it is more open and tolerant than, say, Christianity or Islam, pluralism is logically no different. After all, pluralists believe that they have a virtue the Christian or Muslim does not have; that is, they believe themselves to be correct and the Christian to be in error. But that's exactly the problem pluralists are trying to avoid. They don't like the Christian faith's exclusivity because it claims that where other views conflict with it, at that point they would be in error. But pluralists believe the Christian is wrong. Pluralism is just as exclusivistic as the Christian faith is.

What's worse, in order to sustain their own position, pluralists must strip the Christian faith of its essential tenets. The end result? The pluralist's version of Jesus becomes utterly unrecognizable to the orthodox Christian. Pluralism requires dismissing the Christian faith's well-grounded claims about Jesus' uniqueness in his incarnation, virgin birth, ministry, authoritative identity claims, atoning death and bodily resurrection. To the pluralist, Jesus is no more than a God-conscious human being. Now, if that were true, it would completely undermine the Christian faith (1 Cor 15:13-19). But to allow that Jesus is the Son of God, the second person of the Trinity, would undermine pluralism. So for pluralism to stand, the Christian faith must fall. Yet for all their opposition to Christian arrogance, pluralists do what they accuse the Christian of doing—claiming to be correct about the means of salvation. Pluralists must not only reject the Christian faith as false but dismantle its fundamental truths.

Naturalism and scientism. In Dr. Seuss's *Horton Hears a Who,* a mean-spirited kangaroo opposes the elephant Horton's conviction that small persons can exist in an invisible world on a flower Horton found. Despite Horton's conviction about what he clearly heard, the kangaroo announces, "If you can't see, hear, or feel something, it doesn't exist!" This pretty well summarizes the view of many scientifically minded academics on campuses today. They are quite opposed to the postmodern mood embraced by many of their peers, but they venture into another form of academic dogmatism.

During the Protestant Reformation, renewed emphasis was given to certain doctrines that had been diminished over the centuries: *sola scriptura* ("Scripture alone" is ultimately authoritative and, when push comes to shove, trumps church tradition), *solus Christus* ("Christ alone" is the basis of our salvation), *sola gratia* (God's "grace alone" is the source of our salvation) and *sola fide* (the means of salvation is "by faith alone" rather than human effort). Well, in the academy we regularly encounter the quasi-religious dogma of *sola scientia,* that "science alone" can give us knowledge.

It might help to step back for a moment to look at the broader worldview of naturalism so that we can better see where scientism fits in. Naturalism has three central tenets. First, its view of reality (metaphysics) is that matter is all that exists. Second, its view of causes/causation (etiology) is that all events are physically determined by prior physical events going all the way back to the Big Bang. And third, its view of knowledge (epistemology) is that knowledge is only (or is best) acquired through the scientific method. So, scientism expresses the epistemological aspect of naturalism.

The noted Cambridge physicist Stephen Hawking, a naturalist, believes that science can help us answer "why we are here and where we came from.

... And the goal is nothing less than a complete description of the universe we live in."[41] The New Atheist Richard Dawkins, of Oxford University, insists: "Scientific beliefs are supported by evidence, and they get results. Myths and faiths are not and do not."[42] Harvard biologist Richard Lewontin claims that science is "the only begetter of truth."[43] In fact, Lewontin insists that science must be committed to the assumption of absolute materialism— that matter alone exists and that only material explanations and causes are permitted. His concern is that "we cannot allow a Divine Foot in the door."[44]

Of course, this makes certain questionable assumptions about the nature of science. For example, if you restrict science to only material explanations, then any supernatural explanations for, say, the beginning of the universe or the remarkable bio-friendliness of the universe, will be ruled out automatically. This assumes that an inherent conflict exists between science and the Christian faith. As the philosopher Alvin Plantinga rightly argues, the Christian faith and science conflict superficially but are deeply congruent (fitting together) whereas naturalism and science are superficially congruent but, in actual fact, deeply conflict.[45] How so? Modern science, we've noted, arose in the context of biblical theism, with its belief in a rational God who made reasoning humans in his image as well as an orderly, predictable universe that can be studied and understood. By contrast, naturalism's context of mindless, deterministic, materialistic, valueless, purposeless, nonrational processes conflicts with the production of rational beings who can freely reflect on, study and understand such a universe.

So how do we go about defining science? For philosophers of science, these are choppy waters. However, we think a fair-minded, working definition of science is this: it is the attempted objective study of the natural world/natural phenomena whose theories and explanations do not normally depart from the natural realm.[46] The key phrase is "do not normally depart from." Now, some scientists will insist that science studies what never departs from the natural realm. But clearly, this is a philosophical question, not a scientific one. After all, how could observations from the physical world rule out nonphysical causes, such as a miraculous event like Jesus' bodily resurrection? Why think that science requires all natural phenomena to be explained only by prior natural causes? Instead of asking what is the best natural explanation, we should take this tack: What is the best *overall* explanation for this natural phenomenon? That is, does the evidence point us in the direction of supernatural or merely natural explanations?

The problem with the assumption that science requires only natural/ material explanations is not science but scientism. What is scientism? It is the assumption that the material world is all there is and that science is the only—or perhaps, best—means of verifying truth claims; all claims of knowledge have to be scientifically verifiable.

To go about doing science this way is a skewed methodology. Scientism is a philosophical position; it is not the result of scientific research. After all, how could one know scientifically that the material world is all there is?

Another problem with scientism is that it is arbitrary. Why think all truth claims have to be scientifically (empirically) verifiable? What about philosophy or theology or mathematics? One atheist philosopher claimed that there can't be a cause of the origin of the universe since "by definition the universe contains everything there is or ever was or will be."[47] This engages in question begging, assuming what one wants to prove. The assumption that the physical world is all the reality there is arbitrarily excludes the realm of God, objective ethics and duties, free will, the soul, and objective purpose and meaning to life. Science can tell us a lot, but it can't tell us whether the soul exists, the will is free or humans have intrinsic rights.

Scientism is also self-refuting. By making a philosophical, not scientific, claim, it refutes or undermines itself. Think about this: how can we scientifically verify that only scientifically verified statements are true or meaningful? The very articulation of the statement actually undercuts itself. It's like saying, I can't speak a word of English. We simply can't validate science by appealing to science.

Furthermore, scientism is reductionistic; that is, it reduces all reality to the physical, which skews our perspective on reality. The famed psychologist Abraham Maslow (1908–1970) once said, "If you only have a hammer, every problem begins to look like a nail."[48] And if you look at reality as purely physical, then the only tools to interpret reality will be physical. Scientism requires stepping outside of science in claiming that you can't step outside science.

In addition, as we noted earlier, modern science has its roots in biblical theism, not secularism or atheism. To say that the Christian faith and science are opposed is not accurate. As Stanley Jaki, a physicist and Benedictine priest, pointed out, Christ is "the Savior of science." That is, the unique theological resources of the Christian faith helped give birth to modern science.[49] Even though Galileo is highlighted as an honest, courageous observer whose faith was in stark opposition to the scientific evidence, he himself was committed to a no-ultimate-conflict view between them. He said in a letter to the Duchess Kristina in 1615 that when the Scriptures are properly interpreted and science properly understood, these two books of God's revelation will ultimately not contradict each other.

Figure 4.6. Galileo Galilei (1564–1642) is famous for his confrontation with the church over science, an event surrounded by many myths. In fact, during this time Jesuit astronomers were quietly teaching Copernican astronomy in Catholic universities and were frustrated that Galileo, with his bombastic style, had turned the motion of the earth into a political controversy.

SUMMARY OF OUR ATHENS

These issues of postmodernism and relativism, emotivism, religious pluralism, and scientism are central to the thinking of our own Athens today. We encounter them not only in the academy but in our daily conversations with neighbors, work colleagues and fellow students. Christians must be well grounded in their faith and astute observers of culture—while also learning lessons from thinkers like Justin Martyr and Augustine—so that they can think carefully about these matters to better articulate the gospel for today's Athenians.

5

PAUL'S SPEECHES IN ACTS

Why does Luke include Paul's Areopagus speech in the narrative of Acts? While we could say that Luke recorded the speech because it happened that way, and Acts is telling us what happened, there is far more to it than that. We can certainly affirm that Acts presents events that actually happened, but when Hellenistic historiographers, including Luke, wrote narratives, they had more in mind than simply reporting the facts. And as we'll see, Luke wants to portray Paul as one who masterfully navigated the protocols of introducing a new deity in Athens, a delicate undertaking that required the Mars Hill council's permission. Here we want to consider what else Luke sought to accomplish with Paul's speech. To do that, we will consider the functions or purposes of the speeches in Acts.

ACTS: HISTORY AS THE HELLENISTS DID IT

First, we need to see Acts in its original literary context. While there is some debate over this, it seems fairly clear that the genre of the Acts of the Apostles is Hellenistic historiography. Acts forms volume two of a two-volume history by Luke. The first volume is the Gospel according to Luke. If you read the opening verses of Luke's Gospel in their original Greek, you can see striking parallels to other Hellenistic historiographers,[1] especially the greatest example, Thucydides. He wrote a work on the Peloponnesian War between Athens and Sparta (431–404 B.C.). Later Hellenistic historiographers sought to imitate Thucydides's style.

In the second century A.D., likely at least fifty or more years after Luke wrote Acts, Lucian (A.D. 115–190) wrote *How to Write History*. In this work, Lucian puts forth Thucydides as the model, indeed the gold standard, for other historians to follow. He describes the process of writing history, suggesting that one must report the facts but should do it with artistry. Lucian says that a work of *historia,* which refers to the knowledge gained through inquiry into an event, as recorded in an account, story or history, should be like "well-seasoned soup," a blend of facts, good literary style and rhetorical skill. Lucian never suggested, however, that style or rhetorical skill was more important than what actually happened and, in another work, even mocked those who wrote of things for which they did not actually have the facts. This is important because many modern scholars speak as though ancient historians cared only about their rhetorical goals, and not about the facts. This can only be maintained if one ignores the evidence of Greco-Roman historiographers themselves.

The Acts of the Apostles contains many speeches, as well as other forms of discourse. Many commentators have identified twenty-four or more speeches in Acts, though what constitutes a speech is open to debate. The speeches that Luke records are undoubtedly summaries. Thucydides tells his readers that he could not always remember what someone said in a speech he heard, nor could he always find out accurately from others what someone said on a given occasion. Consequently, Thucydides has speeches in his work on the Peloponnesian War that offer the gist of what the speaker said (*Hist.* 1.22.1). This passage has been the source of great controversy, with some saying that Thucydides claimed he recorded speeches as accurately as possible while others interpret him to mean that Thucydides invented speeches out of thin air. If you read Thucydides in Greek, you will see that his statement is very ambiguous and could be taken either way. Since Thucydides could have been clearer, he probably meant to be ambiguous. Nevertheless, we side with the scholars who understand what Thucydides said in the larger context of the preface to his work, and Lucian's interpretation of what Thucydides wrote, as claiming that he offered the gist of what was said.[2]

Luke followed this practice in the speeches in Acts. These speeches provide the gist of what was said by Peter, Paul, Stephen and others. This in no way takes away from the historical reliability of Acts. However, if you read Paul's speech at Mars Hill in Acts 17:16-34 or Peter's speech on the day of Pentecost in Acts 2:16-42 aloud at a speed that someone would normally speak, neither of these will take you more than a couple of minutes. It is extremely unlikely that Paul spoke for only a minute to the gathered Athenian audience when he had been asked to describe what he was teaching and who these new deities were.

This is supported by a later account of Paul's speaking in Acts. Acts 20 recounts that Paul and his coworkers had come to Troas from Macedonia. They met with disciples there and broke bread together, which probably means that they shared in the Lord's Supper. Paul knew that he was going to leave the next day, so he began discoursing with them or instructing them. Luke records that Paul prolonged his discourse until midnight. There were several lamps in the upper story where they were meeting, making it rather warm and, without any air conditioning, somewhat smoky. Sitting up there in a window was a young man named Eutychus, who was "overwhelmed by deep sleep because of the many words of Paul" (Acts 20:9). (Both of us can attest to having attended a class lecture or two like that.) Eutychus fell from the third story to the ground and died! Paul interrupted his discourse to go outside and bring Eutychus back from death. Not to be deterred, Paul went back to addressing the believers present until dawn, and then he left.

Figure 5.1. Remains of a bath and gymnasium complex in Troas from the second century A.D. Notice the sea in the background. Acts 20 recounts that Paul and his coworkers had come to Troas from Macedonia.

Does this sound like someone who would, given the opportunity to present the gospel to a group that he would otherwise never get a chance to address, only speak for a minute or so to the council of the Areopagus when he had this golden opportunity for evangelism? To borrow from *The Princess Bride,* such an idea is "inconceivable"! Would any evangelist today speak for only one minute or so? Certainly not. An evangelist would take full advantage of the situation. Rather, we should see Paul's speech in this case, as well as all the speeches in Acts, as summaries or outlines of what the speakers said.

Again, this is not a problem because the standard of offering the basic ideas of a speech, rather than a complete transcription as we might expect in a newspaper for a speech by a politician in the twenty-first century, was established long before Acts was written. It is also instructive to note that the narrative of Acts and all the speeches share the same Greek literary style. This consistent style indicates that Luke is reporting the essence of what was said but not the exact wording. If he were reporting the exact wording, the speeches would have quite different styles most probably.

This summary nature of the speeches is relevant in part because many scholars, observing the similarity in style between speeches, accuse Luke of inventing these speeches with no historical basis for them. If the speeches are summaries, however, similarity in style indicates absolutely nothing about the historical accuracy of the speeches. The criticism of Acts for reporting unhistorical speeches goes along with the views of many scholars that Acts itself is historically unreliable. In general, such assertions (not arguments based upon empirical evidence) ignore the facts and substitute speculation for data.[3]

Furthermore, there is good reason to regard the Acts of the Apostles as historically reliable.[4] We may regard Paul's speech at Athens as a reliable summary of what Paul said on that occasion and reject the views of scholars who assert, without evidence, that the speech never took place. All that being said, what is important for our purposes is the function of the speeches in Acts.

Paul's Audiences and Purposes

The speeches in Acts have a variety of audiences and purposes. Peter's speeches in Acts 2 and 3, as well as Paul's speech in Acts 13, are addressed to Jews. Each seeks to lead Jews to accept Jesus of Nazareth as the true Messiah. Acts 7, which is often referred to as Stephen's defense speech, reads as anything but a defense. Instead of dealing with the charges against him directly, Stephen's speech before the Sanhedrin is much more like a prophetic rebuke, in the style of Jeremiah or Amos, for example.[5] Stephen summarizes stories from Genesis and Exodus, quotes from Amos and makes other biblical references.

Peter's third major speech as recorded in Acts 10 is addressed to a Gentile audience. While Peter's speech at Pentecost had been full of direct quotations of biblical texts such as Joel 2 and Psalm 110, Peter's speech to Cornelius and other Gentiles in Acts 10:34-43 has no explicit quotations of Scripture, though it does reflect some biblical themes and refers to "the prophets." While Paul's first recorded speech in Acts 13 is full of scriptural quotations, Paul's brief speech at Lystra, where the audience would have had no knowledge of the Scriptures of Israel, contains no biblical citations, although it too exhibits scriptural echoes and biblical themes (Acts 14:15-17).[6] When James speaks at the Jerusalem Council in Acts 15 to a Jewish Christian audience, he quotes Amos 9:11-12, but when Paul delivers his speech in Athens, he employs echoes of Scripture and refers to many biblical themes, as will be described in a later chapter, but he does not quote any verses from the Scriptures. While Paul's defense speech before King Agrippa in Acts 26 has some connections with Ezekiel 1–3, it does not quote any biblical text either.

The speeches in Acts that quote biblical texts explicitly are often seeking to bring Jews to believe in Jesus as the Messiah. Speeches made to Gentiles that have an evangelistic focus, however, do not quote biblical texts, even though these speeches reflect biblical themes. This is similar to what we find in Paul's letters. Romans and 1 Corinthians, which are written to house churches that contain both Jewish and Gentile believers in Jesus, contain many explicit biblical citations, such as "For the Scripture says, 'Everyone who believes in him will not be put to shame'" (Rom 10:11). Letters to house churches that contain few or no Jewish Christians do not have any explicit quotations of Scripture, as can be seen in Philippians or Colossians. These letters do contain echoes of Scripture, but they do not contain biblical quotations with introductory formulas. Most likely, Paul does not make explicit scriptural quotations in these letters because the audiences for these letters do not have a background in Scripture as Jewish Christians would.

The Mixed Response Paul Received

Acts 13–28 focuses on the apostle Paul. All of his speeches in Acts are in these chapters. In narrating Paul's speeches, Luke shows what happens when the gospel encounters various religious and philosophical ideas and beliefs. On Crete, Paul's message challenges and overcomes the false teachings of a sorcerer (Elymas) and describes the chief political figure (Sergius Paulus), doubtless a Gentile, coming to faith in Jesus the Messiah. Then we read of Paul preaching to Jews and probably God-fearers at Pisidian Antioch.[7] It is important to notice what happens in terms of a response. Some Jews accept Paul's message that Jesus is the Messiah, but others do not. Many Gentiles, however, accept Paul's message, although some do not. This mixed response was common for Paul. He received a mixed response at Corinth and a mixed response when preaching to prominent Jews in Rome (Acts 28:24-31).

Luke's repetition of this theme of a mixed response to the gospel is important for the rhetoric of Acts. Pseudo-Cicero, a writer on rhetoric, advises in *Rhetorica ad Herennium* that orators ought not "to repeat the same thing precisely—for that, to be sure, would weary the hearer, and not refine the idea—but [he should repeat the idea] with changes" (*Rhet. Her.* 4.42.54). In fact, "repetition can make a deep impression on the hearer."[8]

Acts uses repetition and parallels in several ways, including its portrayal of the mixed responses of audiences. Such repetition can assist an orator in persuading his audience of his point. In this case, Luke leaves no doubt that response to the gospel will always be mixed. Some will believe while others will not. This suggests that when Luke records that a few people in Athens believe, he is not presenting a negative picture of Paul's efforts there, as some biblical scholars have wrongly suggested.[9] Luke is not reticent to speak of moments of failure on Paul's part, such as the argument with Barnabas in Acts 15:36-39, but that is clearly not what Acts is saying happened here. In Acts 17:34, Luke makes it clear that Paul's efforts to proclaim the gospel to Gentile intellectual and social elites met with some success. So Luke's audience could use Paul's approach as a model to follow. The theory that Paul failed in his approach in Athens and that at his next stop in Corinth (Acts 18) he switched to a different approach because of this failure does not consider enough factors within the narrative and ignores the realities of differences between philosophers in Athens and sophists (those skilled in rhetoric who spoke for money regardless of what they thought of a topic) in Corinth.[10]

Figure 5.2. A bema, the large stone structure shown here, has been excavated at Corinth. This may be the spot where Paul was brought before Gallio for judgment. See incident recorded in Act 18:12-16.

FORM AND FUNCTION

As suggested above, Acts does not contain speeches solely out of historical interest. Like all Hellenistic historiography, and like biblical history, such as that found in 1 Samuel or 2 Kings, Acts has a rhetorical goal. The word *rhetoric* in a Greco-Roman context did not have the negative sense that we attach to *rhetoric* in our day. In Luke's world, knowing the proper forms and techniques to use in creating persuasive speeches was very important.[11] Acts, both the narrative and the speeches, seeks to move its audience to do something. Like ancient *bioi* (lives), the Greco-Roman forerunner of the modern biography, Hellenistic historiography sought to lead people to imitate good examples in a *diēgēsis,* a "narrative" (cf. Lk 1:1), and to avoid following bad examples.

Before unpacking that, it is important to note that the historical works of Thucydides, Tacitus (first-century A.D. Roman historian), Josephus (first-century A.D. Hellenistic Jewish historiographer) and others like them were intended to be didactic. These authors sought to teach their audiences and to lead them to think or act in specific ways by presenting narratives that were shaped to accomplish this goal.[12] We do not know what Luke knew about the first Christians that he did not write down, but we can be confident that he was seeking to teach and persuade his audience. The main goal was imitation of that which was good or virtuous.

The speeches in Acts are integral to this educational function of the Acts of the Apostles. Luke's audience (not the original audience on Mars Hill) would have learned from Paul's speech both theology and an approach for reaching intellectuals. Acts offers two speeches as models for approaching non-Christian audiences that have little or no background in biblical ideas. This is relevant for us because many people in our culture have only a vague idea of some of what is in the Bible and are far from being biblically literate or able to summarize even core theological teachings of the Bible. The speech in Acts 14:13-17 is spoken to a non-Jewish audience that is presented as enthusiastic and very religious but perhaps uncultured since the narrative implies that the crowd was not very good at understanding Greek (Acts 14:9-12). At the very least Lystra was no match for important cities like Ephesus, Corinth or Rome. Paul's speech at Lystra shows a way to approach a group that does not have a biblical frame of reference.

PAUL AT ATHENS

When Paul arrived in Athens, he was in a city that, while not as important or glorious as it once was, remained a prestigious city. Acts states that Paul was taken to the Areopagus. While this could be the hill called Areopagus (or Mars Hill), it is much more likely that this refers to the council of the Areopagus, which had the responsibility for hearing criminal, especially capital, cases. The council may have met at Mars Hill. Or perhaps it was at the royal stoa—an open building with columns that support the roof lining the hall— in the northwest corner of the agora (marketplace), although there is little evidence for this. Either way, Paul was brought before the Areopagus council to explain his views, not simply to chat about his views with any interested party. And this is his initial defense speech.[13] It is not certain if Paul was simply being asked to describe his views or was put on trial. The latter seems more likely, and if it was a trial, the charge against Paul was probably that he was introducing new deities to Athens, and one needed permission to do this. Paul had not obtained that permission. In this city Paul did not take the fairly simple approach of Acts 14 in arguing from nature. Instead, he built cultural bridges by borrowing from Greek authors whose writings could be used to support Paul's message about Jesus. Luke thus has shown us two different ways to approach a primarily, if not exclusively, Gentile audience.

In both Lystra and Athens there might have been some acquaintance with Israel's Scriptures (more likely in Athens where there was a synagogue, according to Acts 17:17) and probably with the seemingly odd practices of Jews, like avoiding pork and taking Saturdays off from work. There certainly had not been, however, any preaching of the gospel of Jesus the Messiah in either place. Interestingly, Luke does not indicate that anyone in Lystra, except perhaps the healed lame man of Acts 14:8-9, was convinced by Paul and put faith in Jesus.[14] By contrast, Acts explicitly states that Paul had some success as an evangelist at Athens. This speech, like all the speeches in Acts, serves as a template for how believers can, and probably should, orient or structure their presentation of the gospel in audience-specific ways.

The speeches in Acts also serve the purpose of providing a means for Luke to interpret the events of the narrative. This shows up in Acts 1:15-22 when Peter explains how the Scriptures speak of betrayal by one's friend and a wish for the betrayer's demise (a request for God to act justly).

THREE ELEMENTS OF THE SPEECHES

So there are three elements of the speeches in Acts that should be kept in mind. First, the speeches in Acts not only give the gist of what each speaker said and present Luke's understanding of the Way, but they also provide templates or models to imitate when the members of Luke's audience present the gospel to their neighbors. Second, the various recorded speeches show that the preaching of the gospel was presented by followers of Jesus the Messiah in ways that would be the most meaningful to their audiences. Third, in general, there was a mixed response to preaching.

This last element shows up in Acts 13 at the first occasion that we learn about the contents of Paul's preaching and at the end of the narrative in Acts 28:16-31. Those who proclaim the crucified, risen and ascended Messiah should expect to win some converts to Jesus and to have others reject the gospel—a theme first appearing in Luke 2:34, when Jesus is still an infant.

In Luke 2:22-24 we read that Joseph and Mary brought Jesus to the Jewish temple in Jerusalem to perform rituals to redeem the firstborn (Jesus) and purify the mother (Mary) from the uncleanness she had after childbirth, as described in Leviticus 12. While Joseph, Mary and Jesus were in the temple, Luke tells his audience about an old man named Simeon who was righteous and devout and had the Holy Spirit upon him (Lk 2:25). The Lord had told Simeon that he would not die before he saw Israel's long-awaited Messiah. Simeon was guided by the Holy Spirit to enter the temple area, and when he saw the baby Jesus he took him in his arms and offered a prayer that proclaimed important truths about Jesus (Lk 2:28-32). Jesus is described as the one who brings salvation (Is 40:5) and as a light to the Gentiles as the Servant of the Lord (Is 42:6; 49:6). Jesus' parents were astonished by Simeon's words (Lk 2:33). Then Simeon spoke directly to Mary, saying that her baby was destined to cause the falling and rising of many in Israel, and that Jesus would be a sign spoken against and rejected by many (Lk 2:34). Doubtless, this is not what the new mother wanted to hear about her son. Imagine a baby dedication in a church service with such uplifting words!

What is important about this scene for our purposes is the assertion by Simeon, who is fulfilling the role of a prophet in Israel and therefore should be taken seriously when he states that Jesus will cause division. We can see Simeon's words fulfilled in Luke's Gospel. Jesus is rejected by the religious leaders and they succeed in getting the Romans to execute him. As we have already seen, this prophecy is also fulfilled in the Acts of the Apostles, in which first Peter and John (Acts 4), then all the apostles (Acts 5), then Stephen (Acts 7) and of course Paul (Acts 9; 13–14; 16–19; 21–28) experience both acceptance and rejection for their proclamation of Jesus as God's promised Messiah.

The mixed results of Paul's evangelism were anticipated long before Paul ever heard of Jesus of Nazareth. Paul develops this issue of a mixed response at length in Romans 9–11. There is no reason within Luke's two-volume narrative to think that Paul failed at Athens. Had Luke been seeking to say that, he would likely have presented it more explicitly and not told us about Dionysius or Damaris. With this understanding as a basis, we can now look at the contents of Paul's speech and its setting in more detail.

PAUL'S AUDIENCE

The sermons recorded in Acts, we've seen, are usually quite different from one another. Why didn't the apostles give the identical message every time they spoke? They addressed different audiences in different situations, and so they shaped and crafted each sermon accordingly. In the Gospels, Jesus would sometimes mention sin and call for repentance. Other times he appealed to people's felt needs by offering rest for the weary (Mt 11:28-30), setting free those in bondage (Lk 4:18-19), quenching spiritual thirst and hunger (Jn 4:13-14; 6:35) or finding abundant life (Jn 10:10). He approached the religious leader Nicodemus (Jn 3) much differently from the way he approached the Samaritan woman (Jn 4).[1] Indeed, according to the statistics, the vast majority of Christians have embraced the gospel because, first, a relationship of trust has been built, and, second, they found that the gospel met a felt need.[2]

Yes, it is easier to give a memorized speech or offer three or four gospel bullet points to people. While there will be common gospel themes we will regularly tell others and while these may be helpful in getting us started in evangelism, we should not remain there. Some will know more about Christ than others; some may come from communitarian settings in the East rather than individualistic settings in the West. In many Eastern cultures, shame, fear, impurity and power tend to trump truth and guilt. For example, a Muslim will more often feel impure or dirty rather than guilty. Consequently, an exploration of Mark 5—the Gadarene demoniac, the hemorrhaging woman and the raising of Jairus's daughter, where Jesus shows himself to be

Lord over demons, defilement and death—might make more of an impact than a discussion of the legal language of justification by faith.[3]

Just as biblical scholars exegete (properly explain) biblical texts, so we should exegete culture as well to better connect people to the gospel. As we point out later in the book, part of exegeting our culture is to be aware that the Christian message is clouded by false ideas or caricatures in the minds of the unchurched. The unchurched often perceive Christians as more concerned about "getting decisions" rather than building relationships, which leads more naturally to making disciples of Christ (Mt 28:19)—not to mention being too political, hateful toward homosexuals, anti-intellectual and anti-scientific, shallow, and closed off to doubters.[4]

If we want to be more effective at communicating our faith, we will consider the example of Jesus and the apostles, who took the context and concerns of their audiences seriously. When we do so, we will show we are treating them as God's unique, beloved image bearers—persons for whom Christ died rather than evangelism projects.

GATHERING CLUES ABOUT PAUL'S AUDIENCE

What would Paul have known about his audience and taken into consideration in shaping his remarks on Mars Hill? What was Greco-Roman religion like? How would he answer the questions most likely pressing upon their minds? What were the common views of the afterlife that they held? Why would they scoff at the idea of the resurrection? Why did they think Anastasis (resurrection) was a goddess?

Let's begin by looking at what clues Acts provides for knowing about the audiences that Paul addressed. The one clear thing that we can learn from Acts 17 is that Paul's audience, like the audience that might show up for a well-known speaker or politician on a university campus today, reflected diverse and mutually exclusive views about the important questions of life. Are there gods and goddesses? If so, what are they like? Do we owe them anything? Can we get something from them or have them assist us? Do the gods involve themselves in earthly matters? Where did we come from and what happens to us when we die? How do we know the answers to these questions? The Epicurean and Stoic philosophers at Athens had answers to these questions. Some of their answers were similar to biblical answers to these questions while other answers of the Athenians were anything but biblical or Christian.

In chapter three we looked at Athens itself, along with basic aspects of religious devotion and philosophical schools there. In many ways Athens had the same sort of population as other towns and cities in the Greco-Roman world. Many Jews lived in Athens, and there was at least one synagogue there. There were doubtless merchants, slaves and the social elite. Luke tells us that there were Stoic and Epicurean philosophers, and both native Athenians and foreigners, who spent their days seeking to learn new things. Luke probably did not intend this as a compliment, as though the populace was interested in self-improvement or seeking to be well educated. Rather, Luke is saying that they spent their days in hopes of hearing new ideas simply in order to talk about them—more of a leisure-time activity (like surfing the web for fun) than a serious academic enterprise. The questions this group asked about Paul show that they considered themselves already very wise. They referred to Paul as a seed-picker or as one who traveled around collecting rags from marketplaces (Acts 17:18). Whatever Paul had to say, it could not be of much value. In the view of the philosophers, Paul had simply cobbled together tidbits from here and there.

The narrative of Acts presents an irony here. While the philosophers at Athens think of themselves as wise as they continually seek new ideas to consider, and evaluate Paul as having useless tidbits of ideas, in fact Luke's presentation and contemporary sources suggest the opposite to be true. Paul is the one who knows the truth about God and the world while the philosophers he has dialogues with are the foolish babblers. Not only does Acts imply this by showing Paul repudiating the views of both Epicureans and Stoics, but the contemporary Greek and Roman literature from the same approximate period shows that many well-known writers such as Cicero (*Off.* 1.18-19) and Seneca (*Ep.* 36-38) deplore the "fact that curiosity over worthless things is all too common among the people."[5] Plutarch's essay *On Curiosity* is perhaps the most famous text on this topic. This curiosity is an unhealthy state of mind, often coupled with envy and malice, and the busybodies who have this curiosity are continually visiting the marketplace in order to get the latest gossip while ignoring their own faults and problems. Luke's comment in Acts 17:21 that the philosophers in Athens spent their days seeking whatever new things they could hear shows that Luke held the same view as was held by well-known classical authors.

At least three groups of people, then, were at Athens. First, there were Jews there. They would agree with almost everything that Paul said except for his preaching about Jesus as the Messiah, who was risen from the dead. While there might have been some Jews among Paul's Areopagus audience, they are not the focus of Paul's speech; so we will not consider them here. Second, there were those who were very religious and worshiped many gods and goddesses. Finally, there were those who described themselves as Stoic or Epicurean philosophers. Both groups of philosophers would have disdained the polytheism (many gods) of the common people who did not know philosophy. This is important for understanding Paul's approach in his speech. This last group would have consisted primarily of those who were wealthy or part of the city's elite. One has to be one of the socially elite to be able to spend time tossing around new ideas, not unlike many settings at universities and coffee bars today.

In Acts 17, Paul preaches first in synagogues in Thessalonica, Berea and Athens. Luke does not tell us what Paul said, but we already know from Acts 13 what a synagogue speech from Paul looks like. Both before Athens and after Athens Paul preached in synagogues (Acts 17:1-4, 10-12; 18:4). Luke gives us no reason to think that Paul changed his approach to synagogue preaching. As in other cities that Paul had visited, Acts immediately informs us, Paul went to the synagogue in Athens and preached or discussed or reasoned with Jews and God-fearers (Acts 17:17). Luke does not use the normal word for *preach* but a verb that has the root behind our word *dialogue,* which also referred to discussion among philosophers of the day. We may assume that Paul presented his usual synagogue speech in Athens.

At the synagogue, Paul would have found an audience that already agreed with much he would have said. Most Jews would have been familiar, for example, with the anti-idol polemic in Isaiah 40–48. Paul would not have had to argue against idolatry in a synagogue. Paul's synagogue audience would have also agreed with him that God created everything, gave life to all living things, created humans and one day will call all the nations to judgment on the day of the Lord. Jews in large measure (with the notable exception of the Sadducees, from which came the high priest in Paul's day) believed that there would be a future resurrection of the dead, at least of God's people Israel (cf. Is 26:17-19; Dan 12:1-3). The concept of bodily resurrection appears not only in the Old Testament. Jewish literature from between the time the last Old Testament book, Malachi, was written (around 400 B.C.) and the fall of the Jerusalem temple in A.D. 70 (known as the Second Temple period) becomes even more explicit about the Jewish hope of future resurrection.

In a rather grisly account, 2 Maccabees 7 describes the torture and death of seven sons and their mother for their refusal to reject their Jewish beliefs and practices. This account is set during the time that the Seleucid king Antiochus Epiphanes (reigned 175–164 B.C.) controlled Judea and Galilee and sought to obliterate Judaism. As the third son prepared to have his hands cut off, he mocked Antiochus. He told the king, "From heaven I acquired these . . . and from it I hope to get these [hands] back" (2 Macc 7:11). Many Jews believed in a coming Messiah who would destroy God's enemies and establish an everlasting Davidic kingdom based in Jerusalem. Based upon Paul's consistent experience in preaching in synagogues, some Jews in the synagogue would have accepted his message while others would have objected to Paul's claim that Jesus, crucified and resurrected before the day of the Lord, was Messiah and Lord.

Paul dialogued not only in the synagogue, however, but also in the marketplace with anyone who was present. This is a new element of Paul's preaching. We have not seen him previously evangelizing in a city's marketplace, which represented the central place in a city or town where people came together, primarily

אנטיוכוס ה־ד׳, אפיפנס
Antiochus IV Epiphanes

Figure 6.1. Antiochus IV Epiphanes ruled over an empire that included Palestine about 200 years before the death of Christ. He was famous for desecrating the Temple in Jerusalem, dedicating it to Zeus. This, along with outlawing Jewish observances, provoked the Maccabean Revolt.

for buying and selling, though there is a good chance that the Areopagus council or court met in the marketplace as well. In this case, anyone in the marketplace could have heard Paul's speech before the council of the Areopagus.

Paul preached in the marketplace because he was grieved over how many idols, altars and temples filled—even submerged—Athens. So Paul would probably have dialogued with those in the marketplace who were not Jewish about the foolishness of making idols and worshiping false deities. Paul's marketplace preaching included the good news about Jesus and his resurrection from the dead, the heart of Paul's gospel. In Lystra (Acts 14:15-19), Paul preached to an audience that seemed to believe in superstitious deification. They were certainly not the intellectual elite of the Greco-Roman world. When Paul begins his speech before the Areopagus, however, he has a very different audience. There would doubtless have been those present who believed in the worship of many deities, but the philosophers present would have agreed with Paul that such beliefs were in error. We turn now to the beliefs of those who were present when Paul addressed the Areopagus.

WORSHIPERS OF ONE OR MORE DEITIES IN ATHENS

When Paul begins his speech, he first states that the Athenians are very *deisidaimōn*. This word could have two main senses, "very religious" or "very superstitious." Paul, facing a crowd of multiple worldviews, might have chosen a word that was deliberately ambiguous and could have been understood differently by the various groups present. This could be a compliment: "I see that you Athenians are very religious/devout." Paul is beginning a speech that will challenge the views of all those present by paying a compliment to those who worship the various gods and goddesses that have altars and temples in Athens.

As described in chapter three, religion was a core part of Greco-Roman society. Civic events and social gatherings, such as weddings, were held in pagan temples. It was not uncommon for a typical home to have a small altar and small statues of various deities. The head of the household would light candles or in other ways honor these deities. Greek religion had a wide array of gods and goddesses. There were the well-known deities, like Artemis the mother-goddess (known as Diana among the Romans, who appropriated the Greek pantheon for themselves), whose temple in Ephesus was one of the seven wonders of the ancient world. There were also the more obscure deities, such as Hestia, the goddess of the hearth. Most people believed that the gods and goddesses, who behaved much like humans, regularly interfered in human affairs. In fact, the Greek pantheon is well described in a quip attributed to Voltaire: "If God made us in His image, we have certainly returned the compliment."

If a given deity was honored adequately, he would bring blessings upon humans. However, a god or goddess who did not receive adequate devotion could bring famine or disease, indeed any number of harmful things, as punishment upon humans. Furthermore, one did not know if one had succeeded in pleasing the deities until after the fact when there was either a good harvest or drought, good health or illness.

By the mid-first century A.D., past and current Roman emperors and sometimes their wives were deified, usually by a vote of the Roman senate after the emperor's death, but sometimes while the emperor was still alive. Altars and temples were then erected for paying homage to the emperor in gratitude for the benefits he had bestowed on the particular city. Thessalonica was very well known for this. The failure to honor any of the gods or goddesses, not least an emperor, was seen as a serious threat to the well-being of a city or town. Yet, with all the altars and temples in Athens, the devout felt the need to add an altar, "to an unknown god," just in case they had missed one. Paul compliments the Athenians for being very devout, which aided Paul in making the audience more receptive, a well-known practice in Greek rhetoric.

GREEK PHILOSOPHERS

Paul asserted that creation and God's providential acts point to God's existence, goodness and Lordship over the entire cosmos. Paul's speech would have been more palatable to the Stoic philosophers present, who believed in a form of divine providence, than to the Epicureans. For Paul this is natural revelation: you could see it with your own eyes. Paul also spoke, however, about a man appointed by God to judge the world and whose validity was proved by God raising him from the dead. The Epicureans and Stoics would have disagreed with Paul on all these points. They did not believe in a future judgment by any deity, and they rejected categorically the idea of bodily resurrection.

In stark contrast to Paul (and Judaism), the Stoics believed that the way to learn of God's existence was solely through human reasoning, which was given to humans by the divine Logos. *Logos* often means *word* but can also be used for more complex ideas, including reason, and that is how the Stoics used it. They would not look to nature to learn about God but believed that all people have an idea of God because God is the cosmos and all that is in it. They might not all agree on every point about God, but all would agree that "the Deity is incorruptible, perfect, endowed with reason, and acts as a kind of Providence."[6] These insights are in a person's own soul, and they are the first source of the knowledge of God since all people contain and are part of the divine Reason. A second source comes from ideas learned through education or other individuals, such as poets and artists. The Stoics saw a human's innate reason and what one learns from being taught as the primary sources of knowledge of the Deity.

This innate knowledge of God shows the divine origin of the soul and therefore the kinship of all with Deity. The human reason is part of the divine Reason that guides both events and human thought. So when Paul speaks of humans as God's offspring, the Stoics would have agreed with him, but they had a very different conception of Deity from Paul's understanding.

Furthermore, this knowledge of God came through thought, not through experiences of the body. The biblical view of a person as being an embodied soul saw the body as a good creation of God. The Stoics rejected that idea. Following in the footsteps of Plato, they saw the body as a prison from which we need to escape. At death the divine spark in each person returns to the cosmic Logos from which it comes. This means that everyone is divine since everything is God. According to the famous Roman orator Cicero, we are gods.[7] The world of sense impressions, however, does contribute something for the Stoics, for the orderliness and rationality of the external world proves the existence of a supreme being. While Stoics by Paul's day had begun to discuss the possibility of the existence of the soul after death, they most certainly did not believe in a future embodied state for humans after death.

Paul's speech would have been more problematic for Epicureans. While they believed that there were deities, they denied categorically that these deities had anything to do with humans—there was no divine providence helping or harming anyone. The soul disintegrated at death, and there was no afterlife and therefore no such thing as a resurrection of the dead. There literally was no one to resurrect. Since the gods did not interact with humans and people ceased to exist at death, there was no reason to believe that people would be judged in this life or the next for their choice to seek or not seek some deity. Epicurus taught his principles with the explicit purpose of freeing people from fear of judgment by deities in the afterlife.

Stoic and Epicurean teaching changed somewhat after the rise of the Roman Empire. Initially, dead emperors and, later, living emperors, and even some relatives, were declared by the Roman senate to be divine. So religious rituals were developed to pay homage to these deities. This imperial cult did not stay in Rome but was imposed upon cities across the Roman Empire, including Athens. The homage to these new gods and goddesses was premised upon the benefits the Romans brought to places where they imposed the Pax Romana, the peace and security of Roman rule.[8]

In addition, the general populace of the Greco-Roman world believed in many gods and goddesses. In order to avoid offending the Romans and to make their philosophies more acceptable to the masses, the Stoics and Epicureans found ways to include or accommodate these other deities in their beliefs. For example, the Stoics came to call the divine Logos by the name Zeus and said that the one God is known by many names. When Paul speaks to those gathered about idolatry, even the otherwise pantheistic Stoics would have been considered polytheists. Paul's rhetoric about idolatry applied to these philosophers, even if in theory it should not have.

The reality that Paul could not assume every member of the audience believed exactly the same thing applies in our day as well. Before Paul went before the Areopagus, he spoke with whoever came by in the marketplace. It would have been a mistake for Paul to challenge Stoicism to someone who was not a Stoic. Many in our culture hold views that they have merely absorbed from the movies, television, etc.; so it is necessary to ask questions and learn about what an individual thinks. There is no need to defend God's existence to someone who is already a monotheist. There is no need to challenge the general rejection of truth to someone who believes that there are absolute truths. Some people have well-considered beliefs about reality. Others have not pondered those deep questions at all. Some may bring up issues that do not really matter to them because they get uncomfortable facing the real issues in their lives. Others feel deeply broken and do not need to be convinced that they need something. Instead, they might need to be introduced to a God of love gently. Learning about our audience, whether a group at a public debate or a student sitting alone on a bench on the edge of campus, and shaping our approach to speak to this group or this person in an appropriate way, with appropriate topics, is vital. Paul did this well, and before him, Jesus demonstrated it when speaking to the Samaritan woman at the well. Jesus addressed her real issue (Jn 4:15-19).

PAUL BEFORE THE AREOPAGUS COUNCIL

It is most likely that Paul was brought before the council or court called the Areopagus. This may be seen in Acts 17:34, which mentions a Dionysius, who was an Areopagite. The use of the word translated "Areopagite" means a member of the Areopagus. Luke does not tell us why Paul was brought before the Areopagus, but it is possible to offer a good guess based upon historical evidence.

In Acts 17:18, Luke reports that some said that Paul was a "proclaimer" or "preacher" of strange (foreign) gods. The word used for "proclaimer" (*katangeleus*) is the same word that was used for a person who announces a new god or goddess to the Athenians. This person went to major meeting areas of the city, such as the agora (or marketplace), as Paul did, and sought to gain popular support for the new divinity by speaking of the benefits of the deity.

According to Athenian law, however, before a foreign god was added to the deities worshiped in Athens, with a temple and a festival day for the deity, the Areopagus had to be presented evidence for the deity's existence, credentials and benefits. This had been true for centuries but could be seen in Paul's day in inscriptions regarding the dedication of statues to the emperor Nero and to Julia Augusta, the mother of the emperor Tiberius Augustus. So Paul was brought before the council in order for him to justify his proclamation of foreign deities. In fact, if this understanding of *Areopagus* in Acts 17:19, 22, is correct, the Greek text of Acts 17:20 could be translated in legal language in this way: "We possess a legal right to judge what this new teaching is that is being spoken by you," or "We wish therefore to make a judgment on what you claim these things are."[9]

Figure 6.2. Looking down from Mars Hill on the location of the ancient Greek agora.

Acts 17:17-20 gives the impression that some Athenians thought that Paul was trying to introduce new, "strange gods." They took Paul to the council of the Areopagus in order to have Paul explain his proclamation of Jesus and Anastasis, Paul's "new teaching," and the "certain astonishing things." Paul's Areopagus audience was not necessarily hostile to him, but the burden of proof was on Paul to show the court that the foreign deities he proclaimed actually existed. The council members looked to Paul to defend the addition of Jesus and Anastasis to the Athenian pantheon.[10]

That is not what Paul offers in his speech. He offers, rather, reasons why the "unknown God" should not have a temple and should not be added to the existing pantheon. Paul rejects the existence of any deity besides that of the God who created everything and will one day judge everyone. It is the council of the Areopagus, and other persons probably of high social status, such as Damaris, who would be Paul's main target to convince that idolatry is foolish.

Regarding the social status of Paul's audience, let's look briefly at Dionysius, Damaris and the others with them (Acts 17:34). As a member of the Areopagus, Dionysius would have had a high social position in Athens. While Damaris was not a member of the Areopagus, her presence suggests that she too was part of the social elite. The reference in Acts 17:34 to "others with them" may indicate that Dionysius and Damaris were in fact patrons, accompanied by clients, another indication of their high social status.

In the first century A.D., people with financial difficulties did not get loans from banks or assistance from the government. Instead, people, known as clients, sought out people with resources, who could serve as patrons. A patron might give money to a client or aid a client with a legal dispute or other things for which social status and connections were important. Clients were not expected to pay patrons back for whatever help they received. Instead, clients were to honor their patrons in various ways. One had to be prosperous and high up the social ladder to have the finances, social network or political influence to fulfill the expectations of a patron. Clients might well go places with a patron to serve that patron in various ways. In our day, there are people who are patrons of the arts, perhaps donating money to a museum to set up a new exhibit. We are also accustomed to donors providing large sums of money for the building of hospital wings or buildings at a university. These patrons and donors do not receive money later, as though they were making loans. Instead, patrons receive honorable mention in publicity, or donors have their names put on buildings.

This is similar to the Greco-Roman patronage system, except that in Paul's world, patronage was the only way for those without a high social or political status to obtain resources, such as money, land, social connections or grain. Even if this man and woman (not related so far as we can tell) were not patrons, they both likely had high social status. This would also be true of all the members of the Areopagus. This is the first time in Acts that Paul has addressed the cultural or intellectual elite among the Gentiles.

For a number of reasons, religious, political and social, the reality is that Paul's audience, like Athenians in general, had a syncretistic worldview (see chapter four for our discussion about syncretism today). In this context, syncretism is the mixing together of multiple worldviews, philosophies, religions and magic. It is probably what lies behind Paul's letter to the Colossians. It appears that some group at Colossae has combined some Judaism, some beliefs about Jesus and perhaps other ideas as well in order to present the view that Paul seems to challenge. Magic, in this context, is not the sort of magic in which a magician pulls a rabbit out of a hat. Rather, it refers to efforts to ward off evil spirits. Think Harry Potter and defense against the dark arts. Many believed that bad things in their lives, such as illness, were caused by evil spirits. In order to try to protect themselves, people bought amulets and scrolls with incantations or prayers for help or protection against these beings. This was a pervasive idea. When Paul speaks to the Areopagus, he is hitting across the spectrum of his audience's beliefs, although he does not address magic.

GRECO-ROMAN VIEWS ABOUT THE AFTERLIFE

The Athenians had never heard about Jesus or the gospel, although some of its foundational elements were believed by Jews and could have been learned from Jews in Athens. What really got the attention of the philosophers was that Paul preached about *Anastasis*, which Paul's hearers thought was a goddess, probably the consort of Jesus. This was because, although *anastasis* could mean "resurrection," such a notion was unthinkable for these philosophers; therefore, they took the more reasonable path of understanding *anastasis* as the name of a goddess or the like. It was common in the polytheistic Greco-Roman world for abstractions like resurrection to be identified with deities. To understand better the misunderstanding of people in the marketplace and the objections to Paul's assertion that God had raised someone from the dead (Acts 17:31-32), let's compare Greek views and the biblical view of the afterlife.

While Christians take the idea of Jesus' bodily resurrection for granted, this was not at all a common belief in the Greco-Roman world. In Paul's world, there were many different views about the afterlife. If one was a good philosopher, one could return to the stars from which he came (Plato). Or, the divine logos in each person rejoined the great Logos of which everyone and everything was a part, according to the Stoic belief in pantheism. Many, if not most people, held to a belief modeled on the view of the afterlife presented by Homer in the *Iliad* and the *Odyssey*. When you died, you began an unending, bodiless, shadowy existence in the underworld. No one ever came back from there. Once you're dead, you're dead. As a common slogan on tombstones from that period put it, "I was not, I was, I am not, and I do not care."

There was no place in Hellenistic thought for a resurrection; so when Paul preached about the *anastasis* (resurrection), his hearers assumed he must have meant a goddess, since *anastasis* is a feminine noun, and obviously Paul could not have been talking about bodily resurrection.[11] The council of the Areopagus itself had been founded on the words recorded by Aeschylus, who said, "When a man dies, the earth drinks up his blood. There is no resurrection [*anastasis*]."[12]

When the Bible talks about resurrection from the dead, it is always and only bodily resurrection. *Resurrection* does not refer to one's spirit or soul going on after death, perhaps appearing to the living. The dead in Homer's underworld could not be grasped because they were not physical, but the Bible knows only of a future physical bodily existence. While many scholars assert that the New Testament authors meant something else by *resurrection*, such as an intense spiritual experience or sense that Jesus was with them, the data from the ancient world simply does not allow this option. Assuming that Paul clarified exactly what he meant when he used the word *anastasis*, his audience would reject such a horrible idea as future bodily existence after death. Plato had asserted that the body was a bad thing and saw death as the chance for the soul to escape its prison. While many Christians adopted their own variation of this view, it is certainly not what the biblical authors said. The Bible affirms the original goodness of the body (Gen 1:26-27, 31), and Paul looked forward to the day when all creation would be made new (Rom 8:19-23).

Figure 6.3. This tomb in lower Galilee is an example from the first century A.D. of how a rolling stone would be used to cover a grave opening.

The bodily nature of Jesus' resurrection is presented in John's Gospel, in which Jesus tells Mary Magdalene, the first person to see Jesus in his resurrection body, to stop clinging to him (Jn 20:17). That only makes sense if Jesus is tangible, touchable, physical. One does not cling to ghosts or apparitions. This is followed by Jesus appearing to his disciples and asking "doubting" Thomas to touch Jesus' wounds (Jn 20:24-29). To some extent, one cannot blame Thomas for this doubt. While Jews believed in a future resurrection, they did not expect a single individual to be raised from the dead before the day of the Lord. Jesus ate food in front of his disciples to prove his physicality when some doubted it (Lk 24:36-43). There should be no question that when Paul spoke of *anastasis,* resurrection, he meant returning from death in a body, an idea that would have scandalized most of his audience during his Areopagus speech.

Paul certainly knew that this was a likely result, but that did not prevent him from including this proclamation about Jesus in his speech. For Paul, without Jesus' resurrection, there was no gospel, but only worthless faith (1 Cor 15:14-20). We must not make the mistake of treating Paul or the other witnesses of the risen Jesus as naive about death. More than modern Westerners, Jesus' first followers were all too well acquainted with death. If a relative died, family members buried that person the same day. In the Greco-Roman world, especially among Jews, bodies were not mummified, so there was an urgency in getting the body buried or placed in a tomb. They knew very well that people died and that when someone died, that person did not come back to life three days later. This is why Jesus had to provide evidence to his disciples that he was actually raised from the dead in a body. The Christian hope is to be resurrected from the dead with a new body (1 Cor 15:42-49). Paul could not preach about Jesus without proclaiming Jesus' resurrection, and he made sure in his speech that it was clear that he meant "resurrection," rather than the name of a goddess.

In considering the beliefs of Paul's audience, a few things are clear. First, Paul is dealing with religious pluralism or, perhaps better, worldview pluralism. There were those present who believed in many gods and goddesses whose temples, statues and priests were in Athens. There were those who believed that there were divinities but they had no interaction with humans. There were those who believed that all the cosmos was the one

Divine Mind. None of these believed in a future bodily existence after death, and none expected to be judged by any deity after death. Paul faced a group with a large range of viewpoints about God, none of them compatible with his belief in the God of Scripture.

Second, while Paul accommodated himself somewhat to at least one of these viewpoints, Stoicism, where he could, he did not shrink from declaring the gospel or the God of Scripture who was responsible for the good news about Jesus. To do this, Paul not only had to be clear on biblical teachings about God but also know some things about the beliefs of the Gentiles he was addressing. Paul started where they were but moved beyond it, seeking to bring them with him to a different understanding of God. He did not reformulate Christian theology into Stoicism or some other Greek philosophy.

THE AUDIENCE OF ACTS

There is one more audience that needs to be considered: Luke's audience. This audience, which probably included both Jews and Gentiles, was looking to Luke to help them understand how to present a faithful witness in word and deed about Jesus to the surrounding world. Paul's speech shows knowledge of Stoic ideas and the words of the Greco-Roman poets. Luke's critique of the philosophers implies knowledge of other classical traditions. We cannot be sure how many of these traditions or poetic texts were known by Luke's first audience. However, the poets and philosophical traditions that Acts 17:16-34 refers to were well known. Not everyone would have encountered this literature in a school setting, but the traditions had spread throughout the culture in various forms. There is every reason to think that early Christians would have known the viewpoints that Luke in the narrative and Paul in his speech were critiquing.

Some of Paul's Jewish contemporaries had done their best to find passages in Greek texts that agreed with Jewish beliefs in order to use these texts as a way to defend Judaism. A Jew might not have read any Greek poets directly but likely knew of them through Jewish literature. Beyond that, the beliefs of the philosophers and the stories told by the classical poets pervaded the entire Greco-Roman world. One did not need to go to school or read Plato to know about these.

As described in chapter four, Luke is seeking to achieve particular goals in Acts, including giving disciples a better understanding of what it means to follow Jesus. Paul's synagogue speech in Pisidian Antioch (Acts 13) illustrates how those clearly chosen by God to be evangelists preached to Jews and God-fearers. Paul's speech in Lystra (Acts 14) shows Paul's approach to preaching to non-Christians with no Jewish or biblical background who had a rather primitive, superstitious view of the gods and goddesses.

At Athens, Luke shows what one of God's chosen evangelists did when seeking to reach intellectuals, many of whom were schooled in philosophy and believed in well-established philosophical teachings. None of these three types of speeches is recorded a second time. This suggests that Luke saw each of these speeches as a sufficient model for each category of audience. Paul's experience in Athens would show Luke's audience that, yes, Christians should indeed seek to reach the intellectual and social elite, and, while it might be hard to win converts from among them, it was nevertheless doable (by God's grace) and crucial.

It is important to remember that Luke's audience could not go to the local Christian bookstore or shop online for the latest book on evangelism. There were no Christian bookstores, no podcasts on apologetics. In fact, Acts was one of the earliest works by a Christian that offered instruction, implicit or otherwise, on engaging the culture around believers with the gospel.

If we look at the places in which Paul preached during his second missionary journey, recorded by Luke in Acts 16–18, we see that Paul did not exactly experience a huge harvest of souls through evangelism. At Philippi, Paul and Silas appear to have gathered a fairly small number of converts, but before they could accomplish more, they ran afoul of some local businessmen who then turned the city, including the local government, against the evangelists. Paul and Silas left Philippi after having established probably one or perhaps two house churches of maybe ten to fifteen people each. The exact number of course is not specified in Acts, but beyond Lydia's household, and the Philippian jailor and his household, we hear of no one else converted through the ministry of Paul and Silas in this primarily Gentile city.

At Thessalonica, Paul and Silas fare somewhat better. They preach to Jews and Gentiles for a fairly short period, perhaps a few months, and do win converts to Christ, but they soon have to flee without coming close to establishing anything like a megachurch. The same thing happens in Berea. If we could do an actual count of converts that Paul and Silas directly made in Macedonia, it would be fairly small; so the apparently small response to Paul's preaching in Athens is not significantly different from the experience of Paul and Silas in the cities that they had visited previously. There is therefore no reason to suppose that Luke is indicating that Paul's efforts at Athens were in any way invalid or inappropriate for preaching the gospel to Gentiles with no Jewish background.

Figure 6.4. This ancient *odeon* (or theater) from the second century A.D. is located east of the forum in Thessaloniki.

Paul himself observes that in general most believers in Jesus, at least in Corinth, are not in the category of the intellectual elite. He asks the Corinthians, "For consider your calling, brothers and sisters,[13] that there are not many wise according to the flesh, not many powerful, not many high-born" (1 Cor 1:26). While this is so, Paul never says to ignore those who are wise or powerful or of high social or political status. Indeed, he does this very thing in his "defense" speeches in Acts 22–26. In each of these cases,

Paul does preach to those who will make up a minority of those who have put their faith in Jesus the Messiah. Luke provides this summary of Paul's speech in order to show his audience how to do this. Christians today should read this speech for the same purpose.

PAUL'S GOSPEL FOR THE EDUCATED

On Mars Hill, Paul challenges idolatry, Greek philosophy and the well-known Athenian intellectual curiosity. The account of Paul's evangelistic activity in Athens illustrates the encounter between the gospel of Jesus the Messiah and intellectually and socially elite Gentiles. These Gentiles have little or no knowledge of Jewish beliefs and have never heard the gospel preached.

Perhaps you know of a "theological bloodhound," or maybe you are one yourself. Such dogged doctrine detectors are quick to catch the scent of anything remotely resembling heresy and tracking that scent until the hunted heretic tries to beat a hasty retreat to avoid being crushed by the teeth of the dogmatist. Paul has some valuable lessons to teach. Maybe a friend of ours will be recounting the benefits of Eastern meditation, which tends to focus on emptying the mind of all content and differentiation. Rather than being quick to launch into a discussion of biblical meditation, which does focus on content—namely, the reality of God's character and deeds—it would be wise and appropriate to listen carefully and ask thoughtful, exploratory questions. (Just think of how you appreciate it when unbelievers listen to your spiritual story without interrupting at every point of disagreement.) Paul compliments the spirituality of the Athenians, and we should do the same. We can commend unbelievers for being interested in transcendent matters, in contrast to people who are only interested in video games and improving their golf swing. Likewise, Paul at Athens is distressed by soul-destroying idolatry, but he doesn't let it show. He proceeds in a gracious manner in order to keep the spiritual conversation going.

Paul's speech is primarily theological. He focuses on the identity and nature of the one true God, rather than focusing specifically upon Jesus, as in most evangelistic speeches in Acts. Paul's Areopagus speech refers only once indirectly to Jesus the Messiah in Acts 17:31. Since Luke notes that Paul has been preaching "Jesus and Anastasis" (resurrection), however, Paul has already proclaimed the gospel in Athens. This is implied in Acts 17:17 because Acts has already narrated at length what Paul preached in synagogues in Acts 13.

This chapter looks briefly at Paul's theology. For it is Paul's theology, his belief about who God is and how God has worked in history, that brought him into disagreement with the Athenians. We need to keep the narrative context together with Paul's speech in order to understand it fully. In the speech, Paul speaks out of the distress that the idolatry of the Athenians has caused him. The next chapter will show how Paul expressed biblical concepts in ways that would at several points reflect ideas and vocabulary used by his audience. Here we will consider the foundational beliefs that Paul held, for it is out of these beliefs that Paul's evangelism in Athens, not least his speech to the Areopagus, arose.

Paul's theology is essentially Jewish yet heavily shaped by the truth that God has acted in Jesus the Messiah to fulfill God's promise to Abraham of blessing the whole world through Abraham's descendants (see Gen 12:1-3; Gal 3:7-9). Paul never gave up his Jewish beliefs, but they certainly were reframed by his encounter with Jesus on the road to Damascus. The core beliefs of Jews like Paul formed most of the core beliefs of Christians then and now.

THE ONE TRUE GOD

In the narrative of Paul's time in Athens, Luke records that he was upset about the presence of many idols in the city. We should understand Paul's anger as arising out of his Jewish monotheism. Perhaps in Paul's day, and certainly a century later, Jews daily repeated what is called the Shema. The Shema is taken from Deuteronomy 6:4: "Hear, O Israel, the LORD our God. The LORD is one [or, 'there is one LORD']." The Hebrew verb for "hear" is *shema.* Nothing was more fundamental for Jews than this truth. It was, in modern parlance, a nonnegotiable.

It is helpful to reflect upon Paul's use of the word *g/God.* When Jesus or Paul or other early Christians spoke about God, they had a specific biblical understanding of what this word, *theos* in Greek, meant when it referred to the one true God. While Paul's hearers would have accepted the assertion that there was (at least) one god, they meant very different things by the word *theos.* We have looked at the main worldviews that competed with each other in Athens in chapters two and four. As we saw in chapter six, most people in the Greco-Roman world believed there were many gods and goddesses, most of whom were rather similar to humans in their low morals, being fickle, arrogant and self-absorbed. For others in Athens, God was literally everything. For yet others there were gods, perfect but made of atoms like everything else as well as distant and disinterested in human affairs.

Early in the second century A.D., the Christian refusal to worship none but the God revealed in Scripture and supremely in Jesus the Christ led to Christians being called atheists because they rejected the gods and goddesses of the Greek pantheon. Paul assumed a specific understanding of the term *God,* but he certainly did not assume that all of his audience understood or accepted that view of God. Paul had to talk about the one true God. While Paul told the Athenians that he was going to tell them about the "unknown god" (Acts 17:23), Paul does not mean that the Athenians are anonymous Christians (to use theologian Karl Rahner's term), somehow worshiping the one true God/Jesus without knowing it. Nor does Paul mean that he is going to fill the Athenians in on the details of what the unknown god is like. He is not saying that the unknown god is actually the God of the Old Testament without a name or title. Rather, he is going to use his observation of the altar to an unknown god as a way to help him begin telling the Athenians about the one true God, who is not any of the deities that the Athenians might believe in or worship.

Ignorance, not knowing or recognizing who God is or what God is doing or who Jesus really is, appears several times in Luke's Gospel and the Acts of the Apostles. While on the cross, Jesus prayed, "Father, forgive them, for they do not know what they are doing" (Lk 23:34 NIV). At the beginning of

Acts, Peter tells his fellow Jews that they disowned and put to death the holy and righteous One out of ignorance (Acts 3:17). In the Areopagus speech, Paul speaks twice of the ignorance of these intellectually sophisticated Gentiles. He refers to the ignorance of the Athenians at the beginning of his speech based upon an altar to an unknown god (Acts 17:23). Paul returns to the theme of ignorance at the punch line of his speech when he calls upon his audience to repent of their idolatry and failure to worship the true God (Acts 17:30).

The narrative in Acts of Paul's evangelism at Athens subtly makes the point that knowledge of a this-worldly philosophy, including the latest ideas about worldview questions, has left these Gentiles missing what is the most important thing to know: who God really is and his plan for humanity. At the very end of Acts, Paul proclaims the good news about Jesus the Messiah to Jewish leaders in Rome. When he is done, there is division among them, some of them believing what Paul has said, others rejecting the good news about Jesus the Messiah. To the latter, Paul quotes Isaiah 6:9-10: "With hearing, you will hear yet never understand" (Acts 28:26). Ignorance can be removed from the one who has ears to hear. Or, it can be deepened by rejecting what one sees and hears about God. Paul asserts that the Athenians are ignorant of the true God, and now that he has told them about the one true God, they are responsible to repent of actions based upon their ignorance.

Like these first-century nonbelievers, today we cannot assume that if one uses the word *god,* one means what a Christian means. The well-known New Testament scholar N. T. Wright has written of his time as the chaplain of Worcester College at Oxford University. He would arrange to spend a few minutes with each first-year undergraduate at the beginning of the school year in order to welcome the student to the college and make a first acquaintance.

Most students were happy to meet with him, but many commented, often embarrassed to say this, "You won't be seeing much of me; you see, I don't believe in God." Wright developed a stock response to such a statement. He would ask the student, "Oh, that's interesting; which god is it you don't believe in?" Wright continues,

This used to surprise them; they mostly regarded the word "God" as univocal, always meaning the same thing. So they would stumble out a few phrases about the god they did not believe in: a being who lived up in the sky, looking down disapprovingly at the world, occasionally "intervening" to do miracles, sending bad people to hell while allowing good people to share his heaven. Again, I had a stock response for this very common statement of "spy-in-the-sky" theology: "Well, I'm not surprised you don't believe in that god. I don't believe in that god either."

This startled many students. As it was rumored that half the college chaplains at Oxford were atheists, the students might recognize Wright's response as demonstrating this. "No," Wright would respond; "I believe in the god I see revealed in Jesus of Nazareth."[1] What most people in our postmodern Western world mean by *god* is not the orthodox, complete, mainstream Christian meaning. Many Christians might not be able to offer the orthodox formulation of the doctrine of God either, and that is problematic, but that is another issue.

If we want to follow Paul's approach when we use the word *God*, we need to unpack what that means so that people hearing us are not thinking of some other god. To do this of course, we must understand what others mean by the word *god* in order to engage that view as Paul does. We also need to avoid the recent dogma that all dogmas are bad, the doctrine that all doctrines are to be avoided. We need to study and learn what it is that Jesus and his followers meant by *God* and present that God, the God whom Paul assumes and describes in his speech to the Athenians.

The first step we might need to make apologetically is to dismiss caricatures of the God of the Bible (e.g., he hates women, he only wants our money, he is against humans experiencing pleasure, etc.) to make space on the table for the God revealed and proclaimed in Jesus the Messiah. This may be thought of as removing weeds before planting flowers. Paul's speech shows him doing precisely this. He argues to those who would have thought themselves the intellectual elite of their day (ready for named chairs at Ivy League universities) that it is unreasonable, perhaps even foolish, to portray God with a statue or to assume that he can be contained in a temple. For those present who were polytheists, Paul argues that God has revealed that there is only one God and that he cannot be represented by any statue made by human hands. Paul's speech rejects a belief in multiple gods, the distant gods of the Epicureans and the pantheistic god of the Stoics, in order then to tell his audience more fully about the true God who calls for repentance because he is going to judge the world through a man this God raised from the dead.

Paul and other Jews followed their Scriptures in assuming God's existence. Creation testifies to God's wisdom and power, but the Old Testament does not appeal to creation to argue for God's existence. Rather, it simply proclaims that, "The fool says in his heart, 'There is no God'" (Ps 14:1 NIV). Few in Paul's day would have been true atheists, or denied that there was some sort of deity in some form. Many in Paul's audience had the opposite problem. They believed in many deities. Paul adhered to the biblical critique of idolatry. Isaiah often mocks those who make idols, saying that they cut down a tree, make part of it into an idol and use the rest to cook dinner (Is 44:9-17). In fact, much of Isaiah 40–55 focuses on the subject of idolatry and the futility of worshiping such so-called gods and goddesses.

The Old Testament asserts God's existence and contrasts this with the impotence and uselessness of idols (or the gods and goddesses they represent). For example, there is the well-known story of the Yahweh-versus-Baal contest set up by Elijah (1 Kings 18:19-40). Elijah mocks the prophets of Baal who implore Baal to send down fire to burn up the sacrifices offered to him. When nothing happens, Elijah suggests that they yell more loudly because Baal might be busy or on a journey or asleep or relieving himself (1 Kings 18:27). Likewise, Jeremiah proclaims the word of the Lord to the people of Jerusalem, asking them what fault their fathers have found in God that they have turned away from him and instead pursue emptiness (Jer 2:5-6).[2] Jeremiah goes on to say that God's people have changed their glory, the Lord, for what does not profit, gods that are nothing.

Jeremiah next uses the imagery of cisterns to rebuke the people for leaving the one true God for worthless idols. Ancient Israel, like many of its neighbors, relied heavily on cisterns for water. People would dig out large holes, either inside large stones or in the ground and coat the inside of the hole with a kind of cement to prevent leaking. When it rained, water would collect in these cisterns and provide water for drinking, agricultural uses and other purposes until it ran out. If the cistern became cracked or

Figure 7.1. The Mukhraqa monastery on the Carmel Range marks the traditional location of Elijah's contest with the prophets of Baal.

broken, the water would run out, leaving only a useless hole. Speaking for God, Jeremiah declares,

> For My people have committed two evils:
> They have forsaken Me,
> The fountain of living waters,
> To hew for themselves cisterns,
> Broken cisterns
> That can hold no water. (Jer 2:13 NASB)

The Scriptures of Israel declare plainly then that there is one true God, Yahweh, and all other so-called gods are nonexistent.

Paul, unlike us, could assume that his audience granted with no difficulty that there is some deity. The issue in Paul's speech is, What is that deity like? Who is it? Today, it may be necessary to present arguments to modern Athenians that some god exists. This makes things harder for us. The philosophers in Athens would have readily agreed that the worship of idols was in vain. It may be necessary to take a different tack from Paul, though we ought to hold the same foundational truths.

Saul (his Jewish name) would eventually go by Paul (his Greek name), which he took up not at his conversion but when his ministry to the Gentiles began (Acts 13:9). But when he was confronted by Jesus on the road to Damascus (Acts 9), he already believed, as did virtually all Jews, that there is only one true God. In fact, Paul says in 1 Corinthians 10:20 that pagans sacrifice to demons, not to God. The first Christians, since they were all Jewish, were also monotheists. And as Christians, who follow the Messiah and Fulfiller of the Hebrew Scriptures, we need to embrace this essential belief as well. If we don't know what we believe or the meaning of what we believe, how can we ask others to believe it? There is only one God. In modern Western culture, such a claim could be labeled intolerant, but Jesus and his first followers were not interested in what others might find more palatable. (Most people are intolerant of many things, whether they are religious fundamentalists or strident atheists.)

Paul's theology clearly had no place in it for pluralism. Rather, Paul inherited the teachings of the prophet Isaiah. The book of Isaiah, especially Isaiah 40–55, is filled with polemic about the uselessness and even foolishness of making idols. Not only that, but Israel was explicitly commanded, "You shall not make for yourself a carved image, or any likeness of anything that is in heaven above, or that is in the earth beneath, or that is in the water under the earth," which is the second of the Ten Commandments (Ex 20:4 ESV). Paul explicitly states this in Acts 17:29-30, telling his audience that they should not imagine that an image of gold or silver or stone could possibly be made that would really represent the one true God. Several hundred years before Paul, the prophet Jeremiah proclaimed this message, saying that

> The LORD is the true God;
> He is the living God and the everlasting King. (Jer 10:10 NASB)

The entire tenth chapter of Jeremiah is devoted to contrasting the reality, greatness and power of the one true God, the Lord, and useless idols made by craftsmen (Jer 10:10-16).

PAUL'S JEALOUSY FOR GOD

Acts 17:16 implies Paul's jealousy for God. When Paul saw Athens as a veritable forest of idols, "his spirit was being provoked within him." God's jealousy and those who are jealous for him are common themes in Scripture. The command to Israel not to make idols is followed in the Ten Commandments by this emphatic statement about making idols, "You shall not bow down to them or serve them, for I the LORD your God am a jealous God" (Ex 20:5 ESV). That might seem odd, but it makes sense if we distinguish between envy and jealousy.

If you see someone driving a very expensive sports car, or using the latest smartphone, or getting the promotion at work that you thought you deserved, you might think to yourself, "Why does that person get to have one of those? Why don't I get one? It's not fair." Envy means wanting the same type of thing that someone else has. It can lead to negative feelings toward others, but is about being equal to others. Envy is the basis of buying all sorts of things one does not need in order to "keep up with the Joneses."

Jealousy, however, is wanting that specific thing that someone else has, not just one like it. When you are jealous of someone else, you want what that person has regardless of the consequences. If a man flirts with another's wife, the husband would rightly become jealous. He would be upset because that man is seeking to take what is another's. (This is not to say that a man's wife is his property; rather, their wedding vows express a lifelong commitment to each other.) The other guy is trying to take what is rightfully the husband's. If you have ever missed out on a promotion that someone else got instead, you may feel not only upset that you did not get it, but (secretly) wish harm to come to the other person so that you can have the promotion instead. God's jealousy is not the sort of out-of-control anger one reads about in the news at times, such as someone going on a shooting spree after being fired from a job. In fact, the word for *jealous* can also—and perhaps helpfully—be translated as *zealous* in both Hebrew and Greek. Nevertheless, God, though he is "slow to anger," does declare himself to be a jealous God when his people break covenant with him and flirt with or run after God substitutes.[3]

In Sinai, after God has delivered the Israelites from their slavery and oppression in Egypt, he initiates a covenant with them: "Now therefore, if you will indeed obey my voice and keep my covenant, you shall be my treasured possession among all peoples, for all the earth is mine; and you shall be to me a kingdom of priests and a holy nation" (Ex 19:5-6 ESV). God has rescued (saved) Israel out of bondage and now offers to them the opportunity to be his special people. They in response need to obey him and not turn away to idols. That is, they need to be faithful to God just as he is faithful to them. Israel needed to be exclusive about who it worshiped.

Yet, over and over Israel does turn away from God. The Israelites set God aside and put false gods in his place. As the prophet Hosea makes clear centuries later, worshiping idols is spiritual adultery (Hos 2:1-5; 4:12-19).

God takes unfaithfulness to his relationship with ethnic Israel—and, since the coming of Jesus, his relationship with believers from all nations—very seriously. They are to be his, not give their hearts to others, whether Athena, Asclepius or even an "unknown god."[4] In Deuteronomy 32, Moses describes the special status and treatment that Israel received from God. Yet Moses, acting as the Lord's spokesman, appears to predict the unfaithfulness of Israel in turning away from the LORD to worship idols. Moses, speaking for God, says,

> They have made me jealous with what is no god;
>   they have provoked me to anger with their idols.
> So I will make them jealous with those who are no people;
>   I will provoke them to anger with a foolish nation. (Deut 32:21 ESV)

If you read Judges or 1 and 2 Kings, you will see this pattern take place over and over again: Israel and Judah turn away from God to idolatry, followed by God's people being oppressed by other nations, followed by Israel and Judah repenting, followed by God delivering them.[5] Those texts also show God's efforts to bring his people back to himself until, after centuries of idolatry, the hammer falls. God is jealous for the people who belong to him. It is also worth noting that in the same passages, God promises his steadfast love and blessings to all who keep his commandments. God is not only jealous, but the Lord declares about himself, "The LORD, the LORD, a God merciful and gracious, slow to anger, and abounding in steadfast love and faithfulness, keeping steadfast love for thousands, forgiving iniquity and transgression and sin" (Ex 34:6-7 ESV).

The word that Acts 17:16 uses to speak of Paul's reaction to this city submerged in idols, altars and temples is used by God in Numbers 14:11 to describe Israel's treatment of God, "How long will this people provoke me and not believe in me in all the signs I have performed among them?" God then declares that all those who have provoked him in the wilderness will not see the promised land (Num 14:23), which is why Israel had to wander in the wilderness of Sinai for forty years, until that entire generation of Israelites had all died.

GOD, THE CREATOR OF ALL

The second thing that Paul believes and asserts is that God made everything (Acts 17:24-25). However one might think that God did this, the essential point is that God is the origin of the cosmos and all that is in it. Given that, Paul can argue that there is no need or place for temples. If God made the cosmos, how could he be contained in one tiny temple on the earth? Paul didn't have to know about modern cosmology and astrophysics to know that one temple to Artemis or Zeus was tiny compared to the world and the sun and stars as he knew them.

God, however, not only made everything, but he is at work in creation on an ongoing basis. Or, to be more theological, God acts providentially in creation from the beginning until the end of the world as we know it. Theologians would say that God is the creator and the sustainer of

Figure 7.2. Artemis (this statuette is from about 100 B.C.) was the mother-goddess known among the Romans as Diana.

everything. For God gives life and breath and all things to humans, who live and act within God's sphere of influence (Acts 17:25, 28). While the Epicureans believed that the gods were uninvolved in human affairs, Paul asserted the nearness of God, who works in the world for his purposes and is gracious to humans so that they might seek him.

GOD, THE JUDGE OF THE WORLD

Another fundamental Jewish belief that Paul held is that God is righteous (he does not do evil) and just (he holds evildoers accountable). For, "God is a righteous judge" (Ps 7:11 ESV) and "the LORD judges the peoples" (Ps 7:8 ESV). As the maker of all, God has authority over all people to hold them accountable for their response to God and the way they treat other people. Isaiah describes the conduct of a future, coming Davidic ruler saying,

> And his delight shall be in the fear of the LORD.
> He shall not judge by what his eyes see,
>   or decide disputes by what his ears hear,
> but with righteousness he shall judge the poor,
>   and decide with equity for the meek of the earth;
> and he shall strike the earth with the rod of his mouth. (Is 11:3-4 ESV)

Israel, as God's chosen people, is to imitate God in practicing justice. The Mosaic law is full of instructions to Israel that people are not to pervert justice, nor be unjust toward the powerless: "Cursed be anyone who perverts the justice due to the sojourner, the fatherless, and the widow" (Deut 27:19 ESV). Paul tells the Athenians that there is coming a future day of judgment. Most Greeks believed that history was one long, ongoing process, with no purpose, goal or end. There was not going to be an end of history at which some god or goddess would decide someone's fate. Paul rejects this idea and asserts that the Athenians are responsible for their actions as idolaters and need to repent. God will hold people responsible for rejecting the light they have and not seeking him.

Today one often hears the idea that since "God is love," he would never punish anyone for wrongdoing. There are at least three problems with that view. First, Paul tightly connects God's love and God's justice when he talks about Jesus dying for the sake of others, as in Romans 3:24-26 and 5:1-11. For Paul, love and justice fit together well. Second, would we really want a world in which there will never be final justice? The powerless are oppressed. They are imprisoned, tortured and killed. Women are raped or abused by men. Children suffer all sorts of wrongs. If God is only love, but not interested in justice, it means that a child who is sold into sexual trafficking is the same in God's eyes as the person who kidnaps her and forces her to be a sex slave each day. In a world with no final justice, Mother Teresa and Adolf Hitler are treated the same. Some might say in an argument that this is fine, but really, when wrong is done to them, they want justice.

Yale theologian Miroslav Volf was born in Croatia and lived through the nightmare years of ethnic strife in the former Yugoslavia—including the destruction of church buildings, the raping of women and the murder of innocents. He once thought that wrath and anger were beneath God, but he came to realize that his view of God had been too low. Here he puts the complaints about divine wrath or judgment into proper perspective:

> I used to think that wrath was unworthy of God. Isn't God love? Shouldn't divine love be beyond wrath? God is love, and God loves every person and every creature. That's exactly why God is wrathful against some of them. My last resistance to the idea of God's wrath was a casualty of the war in the former Yugoslavia, the region from which I come. According to some estimates, 200,000 people were killed and over 3,000,000 were displaced. My villages and cities were destroyed, my people shelled day in and day out, some of them brutalized beyond imagination, and I could not imagine God not being angry. Or think of Rwanda in the last decade of the past century, where 800,000 people were hacked to death in one hundred days! How did God react to the carnage? By doting on the perpetrators in a grandfatherly fashion? By refusing to condemn the bloodbath but instead affirming the perpetrators' basic goodness? Wasn't God fiercely angry with them? Though I used to complain about the indecency of the idea of God's wrath, I came to think that I would have to rebel against a God who wasn't wrathful at the sight of the world's evil. God isn't wrathful in spite of being love. God is wrathful because God is love.[6]

Third, Paul elsewhere makes it very clear that those who reject God's light receive his wrath. In Romans 1, wrath is expressed by giving people up to be ruled by their own evil desires. At the final judgment, the result of God's wrath toward those who do not know God or obey the gospel is that they "will pay the penalty of eternal destruction away from the presence of the Lord and from the glory of his power" (2 Thess 1:8-9). It only makes sense that God would reject those who have rejected him and chosen to worship a statue or something creaturely instead. Having spurned the evidence of God in creation, and rejected God's love that is proclaimed in the gospel, they are excluded from the presence of the one true God.

NATURAL REVELATION

Paul's Areopagus speech points to another core biblical and Jewish belief. Creation testifies to God's existence. In Acts 17:24 Paul speaks of the God who made the world and all the things in it. He uses this as the basis of his argument against temples for the deity, but this is premised on the reality that there is one true God and he is the creator of all. In this speech, Paul relies upon the facts of creation and human existence to point to God. Biblical writers before Paul testified similarly. The psalmist states that the heavens display the glory of God and the sky declares the work of his hand. The voice of creation goes forth and is heard everywhere (Ps 19:1-5). Furthermore, humans recognize—or ought to recognize—their complete dependence upon God for existence and that they are accountable to him.

The effort to use human reason or arguments to affirm the existence of God and know what God is like from nature is known as natural theology. The value and role of natural theology have certainly been disputed. For example, the French mathematician and philosopher Blaise Pascal said that the God of Abraham, Isaac and Jacob is not the God of the philosophers. And there is the question of how convincing these arguments are supposed to be. For example, are these arguments proofs for God's existence, or do they offer pointers or good reasons to show that a divine Being makes better sense of certain features of the world and of human experience than would the absence of such a Being? The essential issue is whether we can detect or discover something about the existence and nature of the one true God—the God of Abraham, Isaac, Jacob and Jesus, who has specially revealed himself in the Scriptures—through nature, conscience, reason and human experience.

What we should bear in mind is this: while natural theology seeks to work from human reason and observation (without appeal to special revelation such as Jesus or the Scriptures) to arrive at knowledge of God, which the Stoics would have appreciated in their own way, the Bible certainly affirms natural revelation. The attributes of God, his eternal power and divine nature, can be clearly seen through what has been made, rendering all human beings without excuse (Rom 1:20). In Isaiah 28:24-29, the God who has designed and ordered the world even "instructs" and "teaches" the farmer about how to plant and harvest his crops.

Natural revelation, on which natural theology or arguments for God's existence are based, is the self-revelation of God's existence and nature in the natural world and in human experience (e.g., conscience and reason). It would be a mistake to say that natural theology, when properly done, operates by reason alone, as though prayer and the work of the Spirit are irrelevant in helping people see that a good, wise and powerful God exists. We don't argue people into the kingdom. Whether a person moves from relativism to believing in truth or from agnosticism to belief in God, these are manifestations of the grace of God at work in human hearts.

Furthermore, the argument "well, the beginning and fine-tuning of the universe don't prove the God of the Bible exists" is beside the point. After all, natural theology isn't attempting to argue that God is, for example, all-powerful or all-knowing based on the beginning of the universe or the design of the universe, respectively. Rather, it argues that this being is very powerful and remarkably intelligent. Natural theology doesn't—or at least shouldn't—attempt to conclude more than is warranted.

In addition, we can say that if God exists and has revealed himself in nature and desires to relate to human beings, then, it seems, two things would follow: First, we would have widely accessible reasons or evidences for belief in God, and people wouldn't need specialized PhDs to detect these ideas. Second, because God has given human beings free will and the capacity to resist his gracious initiative and revelation, this revelation is resistible. People could come up with reasons for rejecting or discounting this very adequate evidence for God—say, based on the problem of evil.[7] In fact, Jesus himself said that people, if they were resistant to God, wouldn't believe even if God raised someone from the dead (Lk 16:27-31). Blaise Pascal made this point concerning God, that he is

> willing to appear openly to those who seek Him with all their heart, and to be hidden from those who flee from Him with all their heart, He so regulates the knowledge of Himself that He has given signs of Himself, visible to those who seek Him, and not to those who seek Him not. There is enough light for those who only desire to see, and enough obscurity for those who have a contrary disposition.[8]

If such a cosmic authority exists, then humility would be the appropriate attitude to adopt: "God, if you exist, please give me any glimmers of light that might point me in your direction." The attitude should not be, "God, if you exist, you need to prove it by doing X for me." Since we are creatures and not the only wise God, we are not properly positioned to call the theological shots.

Another important consideration is that sometimes arguments for God's existence may become nothing more than armchair discussions rather than the deeply personal and earnest search for God that is required: "You will seek Me and find Me when you search for Me with all your heart" (Jer 29:13 NASB). God isn't interested in detached intellectual reflection about his existence; he desires intentional, earnest seekers. We should remember that even the demons "believe" that God exists (Jas 2:19). They have a justified true belief that God exists, but God is interested in more than mere intellectual belief that the one true God exists. God looks for seeking hearts.

Frankly, a lot of people who call themselves agnostics aren't those who have truly sought for God and have found the evidence for and against God to be equally weighted, which would be an excusable ignorance. Many of them are apatheists: they just shrug their shoulders and say, "I don't know if God exists," but they haven't even bothered to look for the indications of his self-revelation in nature and in Jesus Christ. This is like driving down the highway without looking at the speed limit signs, and when a cop pulls you over, you say, "Officer, I didn't know the speed limit." The officer will reply, "Ignorance is not an excuse. You should have been paying attention to the signs." This is a culpable ignorance.

That said, Paul does not stop with the general picture of God as creator and sustainer of the cosmos but moves on to preaching about Jesus' resurrection from the dead. As we noted, one can perhaps ascertain from examining the natural world around us, whether looking at the beauty of a California sunset or Canada's snow-capped Rocky Mountains, that there is some Being who is awesome and powerful. (The ability to explain why the clouds turn different colors at sunset or what snow is or how mountains are formed over millions of years does not take away from the fact that our world has such remarkable beauty within a larger, finely balanced universe.) The sense that we have of beauty speaks to us of there being One who made beautiful things. The deep longing for justice and our recognition, without ever needing to be told, that some things are evil point us to One who placed this sense of justice within us.

However, this revelation from nature will not take us much past this general idea of a deity who is good and powerful. It will not logically lead to faith in Jesus. That requires special revelation. This is the reason that some theologians have disparaged natural theology. However, natural theology can be an important first step—one which God's Spirit can use—in helping people to recognize that God exists so that they can ask the next question: "If a good, powerful and wise God exists, has this God done anything to assist or rescue human beings from their miserable condition?" It seems quite reasonable that the very Source of our existence would actually bring the necessary outside assistance (grace) to deal with our guilt, shame, brokenness and alienation.

Nevertheless, Paul begins the path to the resurrected Jesus with a general presentation of God and a challenge against idolatry based on what his hearers can observe and experience. This might be seen as pre-evangelism, but it is still a crucial step for Paul to get to God's purpose in Jesus. To make claims about Jesus, Paul has to get the Athenians to see God as he truly is, not as some idol represents him.

Seeking God

Paul also brings up in his speech the topic of the biblical idea of seeking God. He says to the Athenians that the God who made humans from one person and established boundaries and seasons for them did so "in order that they might seek God, if perhaps indeed they might grope for and find him" (Acts 17:27). The prophets and psalmists often call people to seek God with the expectation that they will find him. For example, the prophet Azariah tells Asa, the king of Judah, and those with him that if they seek God, he will let himself be found by them (2 Chron 15:2). The psalmist records that God instructs him to "seek my face." And the psalmist replies in his heart, "Your face, LORD, I will seek" (Ps 27:8). Happy is the one who seeks God, according to Psalm 119:2. The prophet Isaiah urges people to "seek the LORD while he may be found" (Is 55:6 NIV). Zechariah prophesies that in the future, "many peoples will come and powerful nations will seek the LORD" (Zech 8:22).

Seeking God in Scripture is expected not only of Israel but of all people. The Lord promises that those who seek him will find him, and this fits well with Paul saying that God has done good for humans in order that they might seek him and perhaps find him (Acts 17:27).

Jesus and the Gospel

So far we have looked at Paul's theology based on Scripture and Jewish interpretation of Scripture. Both the narrative of Paul conversing with people in the marketplace in Athens and Paul's speech before the Areopagus, however, show that Paul began speaking about Jesus as one resurrected by God. Paul lives out his statement, written perhaps six to eight years later in Romans, that "I am not ashamed of the gospel" (Rom 1:16 NIV). Paul does not talk about God only in generalities lest he offend someone. What Paul demonstrates in his speech is that he begins where his audience is, using concepts and terminology familiar to them. Once he has taken his hearers that far, however, he then progresses to the preaching of the gospel.

Probably a year or so after Paul's time in Athens, he tells the Corinthian believers what the gospel is. The good news about Jesus is the story recorded in the four Gospels. First, the Messiah died for our sins according to the Scriptures (1 Cor 15:3).[9] It is not simply that Jesus died. Anyone in Jerusalem at the time of his crucifixion could testify to that. Jesus' death meant far more than simply the death of a political criminal or a runaway slave. He died for our sins, in order to atone for them. Second, Jesus was buried (1 Cor 15:4). Third, Jesus was raised from the dead on the third day, in accordance with the Scriptures (1 Cor 15:4). As validation for this last claim, Paul lists several people and groups that saw Jesus after his resurrection. The list begins with Cephas (Peter) and ends with Paul (1 Cor 15:5-8). By writing "what I also received" in 1 Corinthians 15:3, Paul emphasizes that he received his knowledge of the gospel story as tradition passed on to him, most likely from one or two of the original twelve apostles (cf. Gal 1:18-19). Paul likewise then passed this tradition on to the Corinthians.

Many evangelical Christians in the United States may think of the gospel in terms of asking Jesus into your heart, but Paul never says anything like that. The good news about Jesus is what Jesus has experienced and accomplished for us. We can be certain that Paul preached this message, the good news about Jesus, in Athens because Paul was misunderstood when he spoke of Jesus and the resurrection together.

God's Plan for History

There is another fundamental theme in the Old Testament, and proclaimed partly when the gospel is preached. At some point in the past, God created the "heavens and the earth" (Gen 1:1 NIV). At some point in the future, God will bring his plan for all things to completion, for God will

> create
> > new heavens and a new earth.
> The former things will not be remembered,
> > nor will they come to mind. (Is 65:17 NIV)

This contrasts sharply with Greek philosophical ideas. For Heraclitus, no god made the universe; the world is not fixed but always changing.[10] He used the analogy of never being able to step into the same river twice because the water one steps into the first time has moved forward and one can only step into new water. The universe has always been, and it is an ever-living fire that kindles and extinguishes itself. Many Athenians thought of their lives as subject to Fate. History had no purpose; it was not heading toward a specific ending.

Paul affirmed a totally different understanding of the world. God made the world with a purpose. From the fall in Genesis 3, humanity gets worse and worse. Finally, however, God chooses Abram, later called Abraham, to be the father of a new people. God will bless Abraham, and all the world will be blessed through him and his offspring (Gen 12:1-3). The descendants of Abraham will be like the sand on the seashore in number. By God's enablement, Sarah, Abraham's wife, gives birth to Isaac, the child of promise. Isaac's wife, Rebekah, gives birth to Esau and Jacob. It is through Jacob that God is going to fulfill his promise to Abraham. By Jacob's wives and their handmaidens, Jacob will have twelve sons. Those sons will be the start of the twelve tribes of the nation of Israel. God will choose Judah out of those twelve tribes and choose David out of the tribe of Judah to be Israel's first king. Through David, as can be seen in the genealogies of Matthew 1 and Luke 3, Jesus the Messiah, the future Davidic king who will rule the earth in righteousness, is born.

Jesus grew up and embarked on his public ministry. Many of Jesus' teachings, prophetic statements and actions were deeply offensive to the religious establishment that ran the temple in Jerusalem; so they plotted together against Jesus, arrested him and held a kangaroo court. Of course, the court decided that Jesus was guilty. Since the Jews were not allowed to carry out capital punishment while under Roman rule, the chief priests brought Jesus to the Roman prefect Pontius Pilate. They convinced him that Jesus had to die because he was a threat to Rome. So Pilate issued orders to crucify Jesus, a death normally used for political criminals, and Jesus died on a cross.

That is not that amazing, as lots of Jews were crucified by other Jews and later by Romans. Something odd happened, however, after Jesus died: he rose from the dead. Neither his disciples nor anyone else expected anyone to be resurrected until the day of the Lord. When the disciples considered what Jesus claimed about himself, and the incontrovertible fact that Jesus had died but was now standing in front of them, their understanding of Jesus and of God's plan was radically changed. Jesus commissioned his disciples to be witnesses, to testify what they had seen and heard, beginning in Jerusalem and going out to the end of the earth (Acts 1:8).

Figure 7.3. The Church of the Holy Sepulcher marks the traditional site of Jesus' crucifixion, burial and resurrection.

No Jews were expecting a Messiah who came twice. They expected him to give them victory over their enemies. Jesus, however, came once to give his life for the world, rose from the dead and then ascended. He promised that he will come again. At that future coming, Jesus will act the part of the conquering Messiah who will establish righteousness and justice on the earth perfectly. In the future, God will make a new heaven and a new earth in order that those who belong to Jesus may live in resurrected bodies on the new earth in continuous fellowship with God, just as God had intended from the beginning. Our first ancestors were created as priest-kings to walk with God in the earthly sanctuary of Eden and to co-rule creation with him (Gen 1:26-28; Ps 8), as was the nation of Israel (Ex 19:6). Christ the archetypal human has restored our humanity and our vocation as priest-kings, the beginnings of the new creation (2 Cor 5:17; 1 Pet 2:9; Rev 1:6; 5:10). In the final state and the cosmic sanctuary of the completed new creation, God will dwell in the midst of his priestly, worshiping people (Rev 21:3), and they will rule as kings, co-laboring with God and the Lamb to guard and keep it (cf. 2 Tim 2:12; Rev 5:10). History does have a purpose.

Paul believed this and proclaimed it in his speech to the Athenians. The story of God's actions in the world, creating it, redeeming it and, at the end, judging it, is so important to Luke that he records two speeches, one by Stephen (Acts 7) and one by Paul (Acts 13), that summarize history from Abraham to the resurrected, ascended Jesus, Lord of all. It is to the specifics of Paul's presentation of this story in his speech that we now turn.

8

THE ART OF PERSUASION

We've seen them on street corners, outside shopping malls and near football stadiums. They're often carrying placards with the slogan "Turn or Burn!"—or perhaps "God hates sin! Repent!" Others carry coins with the Ten Commandments to remind people that they have broken God's law and are guilty before him. Unfortunately, such methods often assume that the biblically illiterate unbeliever shares the same theological background that the Christian does. Not only this, but such a message comes across as merely a bullet point or two in the larger story of the gospel and seems intended to communicate only to believers. These well-meaning believers utilize a one-size-fits-all message that glosses over the particular situation of the non-believer, who may have had a negative church background and goes ballistic when he hears *Christian* or *church*. The advice of James, leader of the church in Jerusalem, that we be "quick to listen" and "slow to speak" (Jas 1:19 NIV) goes a long way here. One Christian writer tells of his experience:

> In a recent radio interview I was sternly asked by the host, who did not consider himself a Christian, to defend Christianity. I told him that I couldn't do it, and moreover, that I didn't want to do defend the term. He asked me if I was a Christian and I told him yes. "Then why don't you want to defend Christianity?" he asked, confused. I told him I no longer knew what the term meant. Of the hundreds of thousands of people listening to his show that day, some of them had terrible experiences with Christianity; they may have been yelled at by a teacher in a Christian school, abused by a minister, or browbeaten by a Christian parent. To them, the term *Christianity* meant something

that no Christian I know would defend. By fortifying the term, I am only making them more and more angry. I won't do it. Stop ten people on the street and ask them what they think of when they hear the word *Christianity* and they will give you ten different answers. How can I defend a term that means ten different things to ten different people? I told the radio show host that I would rather talk about Jesus and how I came to believe that Jesus exists and that he likes me. The host looked back at me with tears in his eyes. When we were done, he asked me if we could go get lunch together. He told me how much he didn't like Christianity but how he had always wanted to believe Jesus was the Son of God.[1]

Crosscultural missionaries typically work hard at communicating the gospel clearly; they often seek to be context-sensitive and use well-chosen words to persuade others. We've seen that this is how Jesus and the apostles in Acts proclaimed the gospel. They did not preach identical sermons but varied them according to their audience and context. In the book of Acts itself, we see how persuasion is very much a part of this apostolic preaching (Acts 17:4; 18:4; 19:26; 28:23-24). Perhaps we modern Western Christians should pay closer attention to their well-crafted, though still bold, attempts to persuade others to embrace the good news of the gospel.

The second-century A.D. church father Tertullian, who lived and taught a rigorous, ascetic form of the Christian life, famously asked, "What has Athens to do with Jerusalem?" He believed that Christian teaching and Greek philosophy should not be combined. Some Christians today have a similar view, thinking that they might be compromising the gospel. While Paul had many disagreements with the Stoic worldview, as he did with Epicurean philosophy or Greco-Roman religion generally, he nevertheless used terms and ideas common in Stoic writings, and quoted from one or more Greek poets who wrote statements that were compatible with his beliefs. This chapter describes the logic of Paul's speech in light of his theology and the worldviews of his audience. By reviewing Paul's awareness of context, we can gain a better appreciation for how Paul sought to persuade intellectually sophisticated Gentiles who likely had little knowledge of Jewish faith, although many Gentiles would be aware of some Jewish history and practices.[2]

We will look at the biblical background of Paul's statements and the way he expressed them in forms conducive to dialogue with his audience. This chapter and the next are not a full commentary on the passage but aim to highlight the flow of Paul's argument and how Paul's own scriptural perspective interacts with the worldviews of the Greeks.[3] In this chapter, we examine the theological truths that Paul proclaims to the Athenians, and the next chapter describes Paul's exhortation to the Athenians for a response to these theological truths.

Greco-Roman Rhetoric in Five Minutes or Less

It's not uncommon for people to attach a negative connotation to the word *rhetoric*. If someone is using rhetoric, hearers may think that they are being deliberately misled or that the speaker or writer is saying a lot of words that have little real content. Not so in Paul's world. In a world in which the options for entertainment were far smaller than ours, it was common for people to listen to orators, or rhetors, who generally traveled from place to place and gave speeches. The audience of a speech would judge the quality of it based not so much on the specific

argument that the speaker was making but on how closely the orator followed the rules for Greco-Roman rhetoric. These rules were laid down in rhetorical handbooks by authors such as Aristotle, Cicero and Quintilian. While Paul's speech in Athens is far too short to see how well Paul would have scored by the standards of classical rhetoric, we can see his use of some of those techniques.

Here are some examples (without their technical Latin names!) of expected elements in proper Greco-Roman rhetoric.[4] Sometimes a speaker may need to take steps to overcome a hostile audience or an audience that, though

Figure 8.1. Cicero (106–43 b.c.) is widely considered to be one of Rome's greatest orators and philosophers.

not hostile, holds a different view from that of the speaker; so the rhetorical handbooks urge orators to begin their speeches with a complimentary opening. The orator should do whatever he can to make the audience sympathetic to his point of view. This may also include the orator seeking to demonstrate that he is qualified for others to listen to him. Then the orator will introduce the topic and state the viewpoint he wants the audience to adopt or course of action that the orator wants the audience to take.

In the type of speech that Paul offers, the next step would be to offer supporting arguments and bolster them with proofs that the arguments are valid. The quoting of authorities—the older the better—was an important technique as a form of proof. If you could cite a well-known writer or orator from the past, that carried great weight. While our culture often gives preference to whatever is new, in Paul's world, tradition was far more important and valuable.

Let's say that an orator in Athens around A.D. 50 was seeking to argue that a certain course of action is virtuous and therefore should be taken as opposed to another course of action that the speaker considers to lack virtue. One way to support his argument was to quote some authority who took this position. (Sorry, but there were few if any female orators or rhetors, even though some young women were given the necessary training.) If the orator had a choice between quoting the well-respected Aristotle's writings on virtue from the fourth century B.C. or quoting the writings of a philosopher who was a contemporary of the speaker, the speaker would unquestionably choose Aristotle.

Paul employs these well-known rhetorical practices and more, which we will highlight as we walk through the speech. By following these rules, Paul could have expected a better reception for his speech than if he had ignored them. Paul did not compromise his message to follow these rules (and they really were rules) but demonstrated his knowledge of rhetoric, which would have provided evidence that Paul was not simply a "foolish babbler" (Acts 17:18) but an educated speaker who should be taken seriously.

Paul's Persuasive Approach

As described in a previous chapter, Paul is probably not simply talking to a random group of philosophers on Mars Hill. He is standing before the court of the Areopagus on the premise that he is seen as proclaiming foreign deities in Athens and that he needs to defend these deities and have them approved and added to the pantheon of deities in Athens. The attitude shown by philosophers toward Paul—"What might this foolish babbler wish to say?" (Acts 17:18)—is hardly positive. So Paul has to defend his views to the

Areopagus and needs to persuade hostile members of the audience.

Understanding the narrative that precedes the speech is important for understanding the speech itself. Paul has been mocked by some philosophers in Athens the same way that they might caricature a Cynic philosopher. Cynicism was a philosophical movement distinguished more by what Cynics did not believe than what they did believe. The Cynics were basically antiestablishment pseudophilosophers. They disdained government, law, social status and cultural conventions, and lived simply.

An anecdote, though perhaps fictitious, concerning the Cynic Diogenes of Sinope illustrates the attitudes of Cynics. It is said that Diogenes was at Corinth, in the marketplace, in a tub or barrel of some sort, and naked. Alexander the Great came to see him and asked Diogenes if he wished anything. Diogenes replied to Alexander that he would like Alexander the Great to move a little because he was blocking the Sun for Diogenes! Besides using the middle of the street for things that were improper in public, Cynics were known to frequent street corners, spouting coarse humor and little bits of philosophy gathered from here and there. Cynics sought to get people to give them money for what Greco-Roman writers generally considered useless scraps of Gentile philosophical or religious tradition with no clear system behind it. "Real" philosophers viewed Cynics as "foolish babblers," the same term that the Athenian philosophers use of Paul. The Athenians are saying of Paul that he is a philosophical poser. At best, Paul's scraps come from one of the many anthologies of brief philosophical sayings that were available in the marketplace, and "at worst, from the coffee shop talk at Barnes and Noble."[5]

Luke's audience has already seen that Paul is a commissioned evangelist, and, therefore, the Athenians' negative assessment of Paul would look questionable in the eyes of the audience of Acts. Once Paul began his speech, any doubts Luke's audience had about his ability to use proper rhetorical structure or about his knowledge of classical philosophy would have vanished. It would become clear that the Athenian judgment of Paul is false.

Using, but Not Quoting, Scripture

The last chapter described some of Paul's core beliefs that were rooted in the Old Testament and Jewish interpretation of these Scriptures. Paul's speech to the Areopagus contains no direct quotations of the Old Testament, such as "in the beginning God created the heavens and the earth" (Gen 1:1 NIV) or "you shall have no other gods before me" (Ex 20:3 NIV). Furthermore, Paul's speech expresses many ideas that a typical Stoic might use to defend his views. This does not mean, however, that Paul's speech is essentially philosophical rather than biblical. Paul's speech is fundamentally biblical, even though he uses terminology and quotations from Greek poets that many in Paul's audience would find acceptable.

Paul is not quoting or clearly alluding to Scripture, but every verse of Acts 17:24-31 is built upon Scripture. Paul is most definitely echoing Scripture. This means that, although Paul does not provide quotations from the Old Testament, his teaching clearly shows dependence on Scripture.

This dependence upon Scripture can be seen when the wording of the speech is compared to the wording of the Old Testament in Greek. The books of the Old Testament were written in Hebrew and Aramaic. That was fine when all the Israelites lived in the same geographical area. After the exile in Babylon in the sixth century B.C., some Jews were living outside of what had been Israel. Because of capture in war or other reasons, many Jews left the Promised Land and settled in places such as Egypt, Asia (modern-day Turkey) and Rome.

Following the conquests of Alexander the Great, most of the Greco-Roman world shared the same primary language, Greek. In order to help Jews who knew Greek but did not know Hebrew or Aramaic, the Scriptures of Israel were translated into Greek. The Greek translation is known as the Septuagint—from *septuaginta,* the Latin word for "seventy." This reflects the story found in the apocryphal work *The Letter of Aristeas.*[6] Ptolemy, ruler of Egypt, wanted a Greek translation of the Jewish Bible and sent to Jerusalem a request for experts in Hebrew to come to Egypt and make one. Seventy-two scribes spent seventy-two days translating the Torah (Genesis-Deuteronomy) in parallel, and when they were all done, each person's translation exactly matched all the others. The other biblical books were translated over time, and this process seems to have been completed by the first century A.D.

Apart from how well this story reflects what actually happened, almost all references to the Scriptures in the New Testament are to the Septuagint. Since the New Testament was also written in Greek, it is fairly easy to compare the wording of Paul's speech with the Greek Old Testament, especially with a modern Bible research program, such as Bibleworks, one we both use regularly.

A crucial factor in Paul's speech is that it uses Greek philosophical terms, but these words are all used to convey biblical truths, not to affirm Stoic ideology. This will become clearer as we walk through Paul's speech. Paul's original audience would not know that biblical statements and themes were the foundation of Paul's speech, but Luke expected that his audience would recognize these echoes of Scripture.[7]

ANALYZING PAUL'S RHETORIC

The following brief outline of Paul's Areopagus speech seeks to show its logic.

1. Paul shows his awareness of Athenian piety (Acts 17:22-23).

2. Paul uses his observations of Athens as entry point into his challenge to his audience's superstition or misguided religiosity (Acts 17:23a).

3. Since God made the world and all that is in it, he obviously cannot be contained in one building, especially one made with human hands (Acts 17:24). Therefore, Paul implies, "I do not need a temple for the true unknown God."

4. Not only does God have no use for a temple, but he needs absolutely nothing from humans at all since he is the one who gives life and everything else (Acts 17:25). By this statement Paul indicates that, "I do not want or need a priesthood to offer sacrifices to the unknown God. They can give him nothing that is not already his."

5. This God made all people from one person, so we all belong to God. Since God made everyone and set seasons and boundaries for them, this means that God is not distant (as the Epicureans claim) but is actively at work among humans (Acts 17:26).

6. That activity indicates that God has a purpose for human beings. That purpose is to seek God (Acts 17:27). This is not an intellectual pursuit only, as the Stoics claim, but a response to God's revelation of himself. God is not far from anyone who will seek him on his terms.

7. It is appropriate to acknowledge the true God by seeking him, for it is by God's power that humans "live and do what we do and exist" (Acts 17:28). We not only depend upon the one true God for existence, but he is the one who brought humans into being, and we are his children.[8]

8. Since humans are God's offspring and humans breathe, talk, walk and act, it is obvious that images of God that do not breathe, walk, talk or act are not worthy of or representative of the one true God (Acts 17:29).

9. God allowed this ignorant idolatry in the past but now calls upon all people to leave their ignorance, repent of idolatry and turn to the one true God. Failure to do so will lead to judgment by God in the future (Acts 17:29-30a).

10. This judgment will be carried out by a person whom God has chosen, and God has validated this person's role as judge by raising him from the dead (Acts 17:31b).

FINDING A CULTURALLY RELEVANT STARTING POINT

Paul begins his speech by showing his knowledge of classical rhetoric in order to win over an audience whose members range from perhaps curious to hostile. Paul attempts to gain the support of the audience when he says, "In every way I see that you are very religious" (Acts 17:22). Those present who are responsible for deciding if a new deity could be added to those worshiped in Athens would likely have taken this as a compliment. Anyone present who believed in deities would have also likely seen this as a compliment from Paul. The compliment would make these listeners more open to what Paul had to say. Paul does not begin his speech by telling the Athenians that they are stupid for having all these altars to false gods and goddesses. He does not begin by telling the audience that they are going to hell because of their idolatry. Of course, even if one knew nothing about the rules of rhetoric, it would make good sense to begin a persuasive speech by not deliberately antagonizing or offending the audience. As can be seen in Paul's letter to the "foolish Galatians" (Gal 3:1 NIV), he is not averse to going in with guns blazing, but in this speech to unbelievers, he starts off by seeking to build a bridge to his hearers.

Paul's use here of educated vocabulary suggests his academic training. He can speak in terms that the elite in the Greco-Roman world would use and appreciate. Using specific language will help Paul in keeping his audience engaged because he will sound like one of them, even if by his words he means something different. As noted in chapter six, however, Paul's use of the adjective for "very religious" (*deisidaimōn*) could also be heard as "superstitious."[9] The philosophers present might well take it that way, as they had the same critique of the common people.

Either way, Paul has opened in a way that could form a bridge to his audience. The philosophers in the marketplace had accused Paul of being a babbler, but by his use of specific words, Paul demonstrates that he is in fact educated and therefore worthy of being heard. By showing that he is competent to talk about metaphysics, Paul positions himself to show that it is not he, but his audience, who is ignorant regarding the identity, nature and actions of God toward humans.

They would not know the source of any Scripture quotations or recognize a verse from the Old Testament as valid. Quoting Scripture to the Areopagus would have been as useful as it is now to quote John 3:16 without taking time to help a listener understand what you mean by God, believing in Jesus, eternal life, perishing and more. One has to establish first that the statements of Scripture should be considered as valid proofs for arguments. Paul does not do that but speaks to his audience in terms that they will understand, even though Paul is filling those words and ideas with distinctively Jewish-Christian content.

Paul builds on this compliment to the Athenians in Acts 17:23: "For while I was going through [Athens] and looking carefully at your objects of worship, I came upon even an altar on which had been written, 'to an unknown God.' Therefore, that which you, being ignorant of it, worship, this I proclaim to you." In this verse Paul shows why he can make the statement in Acts 17:22 about Athenian religiosity and uses his observations about Athens as a way to gain an opening to move to his presentation of what God is really like. Again, Paul does not start by saying that all their idols and altars are stupid. Instead, he can say that among the many altars and temples in the city, he saw one dedicated to an unknown god. The Athenians would have recognized this as true and hopefully would have felt more positive toward Paul because he knew something very specific in Athenian culture.

There is abundant evidence of altars and temples at Athens in antiquity. No one has found an altar to an unknown god in Athens, but classical authors speak often of altars to unknown gods,[10] and the choice between the singular *god* and the plural *gods* seems to have been somewhat fluid. An interesting, perhaps apocryphal, backdrop to this altar is given by the third-century B.C. author Diogenes Laertius. He describes a deathly plague that had struck Athens. Epimenides, whom Paul cited in his Mars Hill speech, had been called upon to help break the hold of this scourge on the city. He collected a flock of black and white sheep, brought them to the Areopagus, and let them roam free in the hills of Athens. Wherever they lay down, they were to be offered up in sacrifice to the gods of those sacred places. If the sheep stopped in an area not associated with any particular deity, they were sacrificed on an altar to an unknown g/God. Laertius writes that even in his day these altars could be found as "memorials of this atonement" (*Vit.* 10.103).

Figure 8.2. Looking across the ancient Greek agora with a view of the Acropolis (left background) and Mars Hill (right background).

Paul takes advantage of this altar's existence. For he can then tell the Athenians what this unknown god is like and, at the same time, show why the altars and temples in the city are not only unnecessary but worthy of divine judgment. Paul's approach here is quite clever. Paul could have begun with a straightforward gospel presentation: "Jesus of Nazareth, a man approved by God, came to earth and died for your sins. Then God raised him from the dead. You need to change your views of deity and believe in Jesus and the God revealed in Scripture."

If Paul had done this, however, he would have assumed that his audience knew far more than they actually did about Judaism, Jesus and Scripture, but he appropriately does not. They would not have granted to Scripture any authority. Homer or Virgil might be considered somewhat authoritative concerning how things have come to be as they are, but certainly not Moses, Isaiah or any other figure in the Bible. That approach would almost certainly have failed. This again provides a model for Luke's audience. They need to help Gentile audiences take baby steps in leading them to Jesus.

Luke's audience—and Christians today—can see from Paul's speech the value of finding something that a listener to our evangelism would likely know about, if not wholly embrace. We can start from there and make our way to the gospel, but as in Paul's situation, some pre-evangelism preparation is needed. Luke of course knows nothing about twenty-first-century culture, but he provides a model through Paul for learning enough about the culture to be able to use it for the gospel. We will describe the specifics of how to do this in a later chapter. Paul builds this bridge to his audience only to use it as a launch pad for his challenge to idolatry that begins in Acts 17:24.

In Acts 17:23 Paul declares to the Athenians that they worship God ignorantly. Their worship practices are defective because they do not understand God's true nature. It is right that they should worship God, but they do so incorrectly since they do not understand who this God is. This motif of the nations not knowing God is common in the Old Testament. For example, Jeremiah refers to the nations that do not know God:

> Pour out your wrath upon the nations
>   that do not know you
> and the peoples who do not call upon your name. (Jer 10:25)

In Isaiah 44:8-9, the prophet mocks those who, ignorant of the true God, worship human-made idols instead. Isaiah continues this polemic in the next chapter, speaking of those who, lacking knowledge, pray to gods that cannot save (Is 45:20).

Paul's speech not only echoes these and other verses on the same theme specifically, but the ideas they express are clearly present, just as many of the statements throughout the Areopagus address reflect elements of the anti-idol polemic of Isaiah 40–48: the inability of idols to speak, see or help; the foolishness of bowing down to something that is made with human hands, especially when part of the original tree was used to cook the worshiper's dinner; and the view that God is transcendent above all and therefore cannot be represented by anything. Paul seeks to correct the ignorance of his Athenian audience, just as Isaiah proclaims to his people the true God as opposed to the idols they worship without knowledge of the true God.

Paul refers to the altar of the unknown god in Acts 17:23, the ignorant worship of the Athenians in the same verse, the groping after God in Acts 17:27 and God's overlooking of the times of ignorance in Acts 17:30. The failure of Paul's audience to recognize the true God is an important theme in Paul's speech, as well as in many biblical texts that may lie behind the speech. Paul's speech then begins with a biblical foundation, without asking his audience to know about the Scriptures. We may think of Paul's statement about making known the unknown God as being Paul's theme, the point he is arguing. Paul wants his audience to accept his view of God. Paul begins with his audience's belief in an "impersonal divine essence, pantheistically conceived, and leads them to the Living God revealed as Creator and Judge."[11]

WHAT THE UNKNOWN GOD DOESN'T NEED

In Acts 17:24, Paul refers to two core biblical ideas: God is the Creator, and no temple is sufficient to contain God. Paul said, "The God who has made the cosmos and everything that is in it, this one, since he is the Lord of heaven and earth, does not dwell in temples made by human hands" (Acts 17:24). Paul first asserts that God made the entire universe—a common theme in the Old Testament beginning with Genesis 1:1, which states that "in the beginning God created the heavens and the earth" (NIV). Genesis 2:1-4 states the same idea. Speaking for God, Isaiah calls out,

> Do you not know?
> Have you not heard?
> The LORD is the everlasting God,
> the Creator of the ends of the earth. (Is 40:28 NIV)

Here the prophet brings together the idea of knowing who God is and knowledge of his activity as creator. Paul likewise tells the Athenians that they are ignorant of who God truly is—the one true God—and that this God is the creator of all.

Many in Paul's audience may have thought that the universe was eternal or that it went through cycles of destruction and rebuilding. Here Paul asserts that the real God at a point in the past made the universe. Since the assertion that God is the creator of everything is so common (e.g., Gen 1–2; Pss 8; 19; Is 42:5; 45:12, 18), it will be clear to Luke's audience that Paul is asserting fundamental biblical ideas.[12] Luke wants his audience to hear the Scriptures in what Paul says to help them learn how to imitate his practice.

Since God made all that there is, he must be greater than and separate from the creation. Paul asserts in Acts 17:24 that, since God is Lord of all and has made all, he does not dwell in a building made by human hands. This is an important idea for Luke, who also shows Stephen in Acts 7:48-50 making the same assertion. Both times, the Scriptures say what speakers in Acts say.

In the prayer that Solomon makes at the dedication of God's temple in Jerusalem, he asks, "If heaven and the heaven of heavens are not sufficient for [God,] how much less the house that I have built!" (1 Kings 8:27; cf. 2 Chron 6:18). Isaiah makes the same point, proclaiming for God that "heaven is my throne, and the earth is my footstool for my feet. What house would you build for me?" (Is 66:1-2).

Both of these texts indicate that, since God has made the heavens and the earth, he obviously cannot be contained in a temple, contrary to the implication of the many temples in Athens. Clearly, Paul is not seeking to build a temple for some foreign deities he is proclaiming. Many in Paul's audience could agree in some way with this, but others would not. Paul tells his audience that they worship God ignorantly when they act as though he could dwell in a temple.

In Acts 17:25, Paul takes the next step in his argument. If God made everything, and cannot therefore dwell in a temple, then no priests nor any form of religious ritual is needed, as though God needed sacrifices. God is the Giver of all, not the Recipient. Here Paul combines the Epicurean belief that the gods need nothing and cannot be served by humans and the Stoic belief that God is the source of all life. This shows that Paul understood his audience's views enough to engage them. We should not act, says Paul, "as if [God] needed something, since he himself gives to all life and breath and indeed all things" (Acts 17:25). Paul's wording looks similar to that of Isaiah 42:5, which states that God "gives breath to the people upon [the earth] and spirit to those who walk on it." The word for "spirit" in Isaiah 42:5 can, and often does, mean "that which animates or gives life to the body," so this word is parallel to Paul's word "life" in Acts 17:25.

Paul might not have had this specific verse in mind, but the verse expresses biblical teaching. Psalm 50:7-13 states that if God wanted something, he would take it himself, as he needs nothing from any human. This thought parallels conceptually Paul's statement that God is neither served by human beings nor needs anything from them. The creation account in Genesis states that God gave the breath of life to the first human (Gen 2:7), and that forms part of the echoed tradition from Scripture in Paul's speech.

Paul is not seeking to build a temple or establish priesthood or erect an altar for Jesus and Anastasis. God as revealed in Jesus does not need any of this. Stoics and Epicureans could both concur with Paul on this point, though others in Paul's audience might object. Luke's audience has certainly come to understand this because they had "turned to God from idols in order to serve the living and true God" (1 Thess 1:9).

WHO THE UNKNOWN GOD IS

According to Acts 17:26, God is sovereign over humans. Paul continues to reflect and base his speech upon biblical texts and themes. Here Paul asserts that God "made from one person every nation of humankind on the whole face of the earth" (Acts 17:26). Paul's statement echoes the thought of Genesis 2:7-8, which says, "And God formed the human being with dust from the ground, and breathed on to his face the breath of life, and the human became a living soul. And the LORD God planted a garden in Eden to the east and placed the human whom he had fashioned there." From him, all people came, as shown by the genealogy in Genesis 5, which speaks of individuals, and Genesis 10, which speaks of the beginning of peoples—"these are the nations of the sons of Noah according to their generations" (Gen 10:32).

Paul's wording here likely emphasizes the "universality of humankind's relationship to God"[13] since Paul stresses that all nations came from one man who was made by God. The phrase "face of the earth" is very common in the Bible, though often in a negative sense (cf. Gen 2:6; 4:14; 6:7; Jer 32:12 LXX). It is used in a neutral sense in Deuteronomy, where God's election of Israel is related to "all the nations upon the face of the earth" (Deut 7:6). Paul's statement that God made humans to dwell upon the face of the earth is similar to Genesis 11:9: "And there the LORD dispersed them upon the face of all the earth."

Until this point, Paul has not said anything that would significantly challenge the views of the philosophers in Athens. This statement, however, would have caused some raised eyebrows, for the Stoics, and Athenians in general, believed that they sprang from the soil of Athens. According to Apuleius, "the Athenians are sprung from their own soil."[14] The Greeks thought of themselves as superior to other people, whom they called *barbaros* (barbarians), non-Greek speakers. Paul challenges this high view the Athenians held of themselves when he declares that God "made from one person every nation of humankind" (Acts 17:26). By this assertion, Paul prepares for his later assertion that all people are equally God's offspring and that all people will face God's future judgment. Paul has not only referred to the Athenians' ignorance but challenged their pride in having come from the soil of Athens.

Paul next says that God has "determined fixed times and the boundaries of their dwelling place" (Acts 17:26). God is in control of the seasons and has set the boundaries of where people live. Their epochs and geographic boundaries are determined by God. Again, biblical themes can be seen in Paul's words. In addition to Genesis 10, which describes the boundaries of nations, the thought of Acts 17:26 is expressed in Deuteronomy 32:8: "For the most high divided the nations as he separated the sons of Adam; he established regions for the nations." This probably refers to the earth's land surfaces, not to geopolitical borders. Paul's statements reflect the scriptural affirmation that God created humans from one man and God established the time periods, the seasons and boundaries for nations.

To many Greeks, existence was simply what is—like the philosopher Bertrand Russell once said about the universe: it's just there, and that's all. The philosophers spoke of how best to live, and encouraged virtue, but they did not speak about God's ongoing purposes for humans. Paul asserts that God had a purpose for creation, and for establishing the nations beyond mere human existence. According to Acts 17:27, this purpose for God's ordering of creation is that people "might seek God, if perhaps indeed they might grope for and find him, though he is not far away from each one of us." God intends for humans to seek for him with the intention that they will find him. About four hundred years after Paul's speech, the famous Christian theologian Augustine of Hippo addressed God in his *Confessions* saying, "You have made us for yourself, and our hearts are restless until they find their rest in you" (1.1.1).

The Old Testament speaks often of seeking and finding God. Israel is told many times to seek the Lord.[15] The same vocabulary and concept are seen when Moses tells the people that if they seek God in their time of trouble because they have forsaken God, they will find him (Deut 4:29). The books of 1 and 2 Chronicles refer to seeking God several times—for example, "now give your hearts and souls to seek the LORD your God" (1 Chron 22:19). Using the same key verbs as Paul does, Solomon is told to seek God with all his heart and he will find him (1 Chron 28:9).[16] The psalmists also call for people to seek God.[17] Psalm 119:2 pronounces blessing on those who seek God, while Psalm 10:4 condemns sinners who do not (cf. Deut 4:29). Psalm 14:2 expresses an idea similar to Acts 17:27 when it says that God looks for people who seek him.

The prophets of Israel also call upon people to seek God. Through Isaiah, God calls people to seek him while he may be found (Is 55:6). In Isaiah 58:2, God rebukes those who seek him with wrong motives. The implication of this verse is that seeking God and drawing near to him is a good thing, even though Israel is only doing so superficially. Hosea prophesies that Israel will repent of its idolatry and return to God and seek him (Hos 3:5). Amos calls on Israel to seek God (Amos 5:6). Paul's words echo the words of Israel's prophets in directing the Athenians to seek God.

Acts 17:27 provides an excellent example of Paul's approach to these educated Gentiles. Paul says that God created people to seek for God, but he describes this seeking by saying, "if perhaps indeed they might grope for and find him." The Stoics present would have accepted this and agreed with Paul's words, but not Paul's meaning. For the Stoics and Epicureans, metaphysics, or the nature of reality, was discerned through the use of human reason. The

Stoics understood this to mean that the universe was ordered by the divine Logos, Reason. Humans could learn about the existence and nature of this Reason by examining their own thoughts and by observing nature. The Stoics sought for the divine Reason with their mental abilities only. They had a natural theology built primarily through their reasoning about what they perceived inside themselves and the natural world outside (we described this in chapter seven). The Stoics were not looking for supernatural revelation; they saw themselves as being part of the divine mind, not observers that needed any sort of special revelation.

While Paul saw nature as a source of knowledge about God, this only happened because God chose to reveal himself to humans. Any truths about God that might be learned from nature were seen by Paul as a matter of God revealing himself through it. The Stoics sought for God within themselves. Paul affirms the biblical theme of seeking God and finding him because God makes himself known. When Paul talks about humans groping for God and that by this groping they might find him, Paul gives the impression that the search by a human for God is likely to fail if they only use their own powers of reasoning.

The double meaning of Paul's next words, "though he is not far away from each one of us" (Acts 17:27), functions the same way. Paul is stating the biblical truth that God is near to people. Stoics also believed this. For Paul, however, God is transcendent and separate from his creation. The Stoics saw God as near to them because they perceived themselves to be part of the divine mind. The Old Testament speaks of God's presence or his attention to people in several different ways. Enoch "walked with God" (Gen 5:22). God "was with [Ishmael]" (Gen 21:20). God promised to Isaac that, "I am the God of your father Abraham. Do not be afraid. I am with you. I will bless you" (Gen 26:24). Moses spent time with God, and the Lord spoke with him on Mount Sinai (Ex 34:28-29). The psalmist declares,

> But as for me, it is good to be near God.
> > I have made the Sovereign LORD my refuge;
> > I will tell of all your deeds. (Ps 73:28 NIV)

The author of Lamentations says to God in prayer, "You came near on the day I called you" (Lam 3:57 NET). After King Asa had won a battle against

Ethiopia by God's help, God's Spirit came upon Azariah, who went to Asa and said to him, "Listen to me, Asa and all Judah and Benjamin! The LORD is with you when you are loyal to him. If you seek him, he will respond to you" (2 Chron 15:2 NET).

Paul can use language that members of his audience would use, but he means something totally different, and totally biblical. The Old Testament presents seeking for God as both a matter of the will and a matter of the intellect. One has to choose to seek for God, and one should use the mind in the process. The Bible does not encourage only the experience of emotions in seeking God.

Acts 17:28 shows Paul citing one or two Greek poets. By doing this, Paul follows a recommended practice of classical rhetoric. As noted above, citing some authoritative writing from the past was an important form of proof, evidence that supports a thesis. This is a very distinctive element in Paul's speech. This happens nowhere else in Acts, but Paul does quote secular writers in his letters, such as in 1 Corinthians 15:33, "Bad company corrupts good morals."[18] In Titus 1:12 he quotes the fifth-century B.C. poet Epimenides as saying that, "Cretans are always liars, evil beasts, gluttons, lazy." These quotations show that Paul was educated and could quote well-known texts and sayings.

Paul did not avoid secular culture, ignoring classical texts or philosophy or rhetoric. Nor did Paul confine his learning to Jewish/biblical topics such that he could lecture on the theology of the book of Psalms but was ignorant of Plato. Paul had studied Greco-Roman literature to some extent, which enabled him to use it when it would help him make a case for the gospel. Paul appears in general to follow the pattern of a regular Stoic defense of its beliefs, but he clearly does not mean what the Stoics meant.

The fact that Paul uses texts from Greek poets to validate his argument is what is really important, but scholars have sought to determine whom Paul is quoting. The first question that scholars have addressed is whether Paul's statement, "for by him we live and do what we do and exist" (Acts 17:28), is a quotation or not.[19] According to the early Christian writer Clement of Alexandria, this is indeed a quotation and comes from the Greek poet Epimenides.[20] The source of the quotation appears to have been the *Cretica* by Epimenides, which is known only from a manuscript written in Syriac many centuries after Paul's life. Epimenides is responding to a Cretan lie that Zeus was mortal. In response, Epimenides said to Zeus that he is not dead, but lives always, "for in you we live and move and exist." Paul says of his quotations, "as some of your own poets have said" (Acts 17:28). While not all Athenians would have considered all philosophers authoritative, people still granted some authority to the ancient poets.

Figure 8.3. This temple to Zeus in Athens was started in the sixth century B.C. and finished in the second century A.D. Paul used Stoic quotations about Zeus, the chief of all the gods, to persuade his audience in Athens.

Paul's next quotation, "for we are his offspring" (Acts 17:28), is attributed by most scholars to Aratus, who wrote "we are his offspring" at the beginning of a (Stoic) poem on the constellations entitled *Phaenomena*.[21] When Aratus wrote that "we are his offspring," he meant that the universal Reason infuses everything, and therefore humans could be called offspring of it. A similar idea is seen in a *Hymn to Zeus* by Cleanthes (third century B.C.), which says, "Unto you may all flesh speak, for we are your offspring." In this poem as well, humans are the offspring of Zeus because Zeus, divine Reason, is part of everything. Paul used these Stoic quotations in part because they say something that would aid Paul in his argument against idolatry, but Paul also uses them because he can fill them with his own Christian-Jewish meaning.

Paul believed that humans, and indeed all things, exist by God's power. Humans have life and are able to act by God's providence. This providence exemplifies God as Sustainer. God has created in the past. Now God sustains the existence of the cosmos on an ongoing basis. For Paul, God created an original human, and from that human comes all other humans. In the sense that God has created humans, we are then God's offspring, his children.[22] We might say in modern terminology that Paul has co-opted Stoic compositions for his own purposes. Paul's ability to cite these two poets should also demonstrate that he is no uneducated babbler. When Paul connects the quotation(s) to "some of your own poets," he is not merely asserting the origin of the quotations. The specific language that Paul uses should rather be taken as emphatic. He is saying, "I am quoting your very own poets, so you cannot deny what I am saying." This is a rhetorical move that challenges the Athenians to accept Paul's proof for his argument.

We do not know where or how Paul learned about these philosophers and the contents of their compositions. It is entirely possible that Paul had studied rhetoric while in Tarsus, given that it was one of the greatest university towns of his day. There is another option, however, that is worth considering for a moment. Paul's theology as it is reflected in Acts and his letters shows, as described in chapter seven, that Paul was steeped in Scripture as God's revelation to humans, but he encountered that revelation in part by being raised Jewish. That is, Paul did not come to the Old Testament with a blank mind. Rather, he read it through the lens of Judaism. Although there was certainly some variation among Jewish groups over how to interpret the Bible, nevertheless there was much held in common among all Jews.

As described in chapter five, the Jews were pure monotheists. They did not think there were levels of gods. There was only one God, the LORD (Yahweh). Jews in the Second Temple period found themselves surrounded by neighbors who practiced idolatry. As for Western Christians today, there were various responses to Gentile religions and philosophies. One response was for Jews to search through Greco-Roman writings and find texts that could be used in Jewish writings that defended Judaism's monotheism and morality against religious and ethical beliefs of Gentile unbelievers. We have examples of such texts from Aristobulus, Josephus and Philo. It was very powerful to be able to say to Gentiles, "Your own writers have said X, which is what we also believe." This means that Jews, before there were any Christians, had taken the approach that Paul demonstrates in Athens of citing Greek authors as rhetorical proofs in order to support and defend Jewish beliefs and practices as superior to Gentile religions and morality. So, while we do not have a Jewish text from before Paul's day that quotes Epimenides or Aratus, he might have learned about them through such texts. Paul had probably heard or read the writings of other Jews who demonstrated a similar strategy to his own.

ACTING ON THE TRUTH

When someone goes to see a doctor for some health issue, the doctor (at least in theory!) examines the patient and describes to the patient what symptoms have been found and what those symptoms indicate. Often, the doctor will then write out a prescription for the patient to take to a pharmacist. The purpose for the prescription is to cure the condition indicated by the doctor's examination and diagnosis. In the same way, chapter seven focused on Paul's description of the nature of reality from a theological perspective. This chapter focuses on Paul's prescription for the Athenians' worldview "illness."

Since Paul could not have given this speech without a knowledge of Athenian philosophy and religion, the chapter concludes by returning to Tertullian's question about the relation of Christian faith and philosophy—Jerusalem and Athens. In order to reach today's Athenians with the gospel, a good grasp of philosophy can be very helpful since we need to understand their worldview perspectives. They should not be asked to believe Tertullian's dictum—that the gospel "is certain, because it is impossible" (*certum est, quia impossibile*)—in order to place their trust in Jesus Christ.[1] Tertullian certainly did not get that idea from Paul, who gives a learned presentation in Greek philosophical clothing of fundamental Christian truths about God and his action in the world through Jesus the Messiah.

The chapter challenges the Christian anti-intellectualism in some quarters. In this speech at Athens, Paul demonstrated what he later told the believers at Corinth. There is a battle going on: "The weapons we fight with are not the weapons of the world. On the contrary, they have divine power to demolish strongholds. We demolish arguments and every pretension that sets itself up against the knowledge of God, and we take captive every thought to make it obedient to Christ" (2 Cor 10:4-5 NIV). Paul first used the language of the philosophers and poets to challenge his audience's beliefs and then challenged them to act on this new knowledge concerning the unknown God.

THE UNKNOWN GOD CANNOT BE REPRESENTED BY LIFELESS IDOLS

Paul has argued that God made everything and that all people come from the one person that he created. People are the offspring of God. If this is so, and humans cannot be adequately represented by a statue of gold, silver or stone, it is inappropriate to think that the divine nature could be displayed in gold, silver or stones, the work of men's hands. If this is the case, then obviously (supposed) images of God are not appropriate.

While Paul would affirm that humans are made in God's image (cf. Gen 1:26-27), that is not his point in Acts 17:29. We are God's offspring because God is our creator. Like God, we are personal agents who can see, hear and speak. Statues fashioned by human hands are not able to do anything, so they cannot possibly represent God properly. Paul's word for something fashioned by human hands implicitly contrasts to humans being made in God's image, but that is not Paul's argument here.

Let's summarize the steps of Paul's argument to this point. He has argued that temples built with human hands are unsuitable for and not needed by God. Therefore, Paul does not need permission to build a temple in Athens. Then Paul asserts that God needs nothing; so Paul does not need any priests or other people for service to God. Then Paul declares that idols are nothing; so no altars or statues are needed for the one true (unknown) God. If the Areopagus was expecting Paul to argue for introducing foreign gods to the Athenian pantheon, they were mistaken. Not only did Paul not ask for Jesus (or Anastasis) to be added to the deities honored in Athens, but by this point, Paul has implicitly invalidated the entire Athenian pantheon. There is only one God, and he truly is the unknown God. God, according to Paul, has acted providentially in history, and it is by means of his favor and power that the Athenians have existence at all. At this point in Paul's speech, he has probably lost agreement by Epicureans with what he has to say, but they, like the Stoics present, would agree with Paul about not needing idols to honor any deity.

Paul's choice of vocabulary here illustrates his approach of using the language of his audience. The word that Paul uses for "divine nature" is *theion.* While this term is used by many Greek authors (e.g., Lucian and Epictetus), as well as Jewish authors (e.g., Philo and Josephus) seeking to connect with Hellenistic audiences, this word is never used by Paul in his letters or elsewhere in Acts.[2] In his letters, Paul uses only the noun *theos,* a very common biblical word for "G/god," never the more abstract *theion* for God.[3] The Stoics present would have been satisfied with this word since god for them was not a being you could interact with but Divine Reason. So this word choice again shows Paul using what he can of his audience's culture without saying anything that compromises the gospel.

Acts 17:29 resonates with biblical ideas, especially the anti-idol polemic in the Old Testament. Moses tells the Israelites that in the future, "they will serve other gods, the work of the hands of humans, wood and stone, which will not see and will never hear nor eat nor smell" (Deut 4:28). The psalmist presents a similar picture to Paul's:

> God is in the heavens. . . .
> Their idols of silver and gold
> Are the work of the hands of humans.
> They have a mouth but do not speak.
> They have eyes but do not see.
> They have ears but do not hear.
> They have a nose but do not smell.
> They have hands but do not feel,
> Feet but do not walk.
> They do not make a sound in their throat. (Ps 115:3-7)

The logic of Acts 17:29 is based on a sequence of assertions, some left unstated. First, humans are God's offspring. Since humans are the works of God, nothing that humans can make can represent God. If this is so, then nothing that such lesser beings can make can equal or represent the superior God who made them. Since humans are made in the image of God, and humans are not like any material thing, God is not like any material representation, be it stone, silver or gold, all of which are lesser than humans.

Paul's statement especially echoes the anti-idol polemic of Isaiah. For example, Isaiah 40:18-20 says that no likeness can be made of God: "To what will you liken the Lord, and to what likeness will you liken him?" Like Paul, Isaiah asserts that gold and silver are used for idols (Is 40:18-19) but should not be used for the true God.[4] Isaiah 44:19 particularly mocks the construction of idols, noting that one who builds idols cuts down a tree and uses half of the tree for fire to cook his dinner and the other half of the tree to make an idol. Such an idol is obviously not a real god or worthy of the homage due the one true God.

Although in the final chapter we'll look at some modern-day idolatries, we can say here that Paul has shown that the idols in Athens cannot represent the one true God. Having done so, Paul introduces the consequences in Acts 17:30. The Athenians listening to him, indeed all people, need to put away their ignorance of the one true (unknown) God and repent of idolatry.

ACCOUNTABLE FOR FALSE BELIEFS

With Acts 17:30 Paul gets to his core assertion. The false notions of deities, that there are many of them, that they need temples, that they can be represented with idols, must all be rejected. Paul takes up the theme of ignorance. He tells them that in the past, "God had . . . disregarded the times of ignorance" (Acts 17:30). The Athenians neither knew the true God, because he was to them an "unknown god," nor did they honor him properly. An altar to "an unknown god" will not do. Asserting that people, including the Athenians, were ignorant about the nature of reality and deity would have been offensive to residents of the city where Greek philosophy had its birth. The Athenians saw themselves as anything but ignorant.

In the past, God did not hold people accountable for not knowing who the true God is. That has all changed now. God is holding "all people everywhere" (Acts 17:30) accountable for their incorrect worldviews. They must repent of their false views and the actions that flow from these false views. The verb that Paul uses for "repent" can mean to "change one's mind" as well as to "stop some practice." The repentance that the true God seeks from humans requires both. We all live out what we really believe deep down. If your fundamental beliefs about the nature of reality change, then how you live will change. If you change your actions but your mind has not been truly transformed (Rom 12:2), you have not truly changed. This is like getting a gym membership or starting a new diet because your doctor said to do it; if you do not really believe that the exercise or diet is really important or lack confidence that it will help you, you will probably give up the diet regimen in a short time.

The Athenians need to change their minds about what or who God really is and what he expects of humans. While the word *repent* in our day has negative associations with street-corner preachers threatening pass-ersby with hell because of their sins, Paul is simply telling the Athenians that they do not in fact know the truth, that the one true God is now holding them accountable for their ignorance and that they need to change what they think.

Since most Athenians probably had a worldview that included some Greek religion, some Greek philosophy and some magic, Paul has now stepped on everyone's toes. He has told Epicureans that the one true God is not some distant being who exists in perfection and is disinterested in human affairs. Rather, he is personally involved in human affairs and holds humans responsible for whom or what they worship. He has told the Stoics that the one true God is not some pantheistic, impersonal Reason. He is a Being separate from humans, who are his creation. Paul has told everyone that idolatry does not make sense, a bold statement in a city where many residents saw themselves as the intellectual superiors to people elsewhere. Belief in gods and goddesses is misguided and false, and the many temples and altars and priests and priestesses for the Athenian pantheon are mean-ingless as well. In other words, no one in the audience, except any Jews present, has been left out by Paul's challenge to his audience to repent, to change his thinking. In the next verse Paul will give a proof for this need to change their minds.

In good rhetorical fashion, Paul has saved his most controversial point for last. In Acts 17:31, he says two things that no Athenian would say. First, God will judge all people in the future. Second, this judgment will be done by a man whom God raised from the dead. As described earlier, Epicureans believed that at death the body and soul disintegrated; there was no afterlife. The Stoics expected the divine spark in themselves to be reunited with the divine Logos. The Stoics themselves as individuals would cease to exist at death. Those who believed in the deities of the Greek pantheon expected there to be an afterlife, but it was not based on one's earthly life. Everyone became a shadowy figure in the underworld. The Platonists, who believed that they were made of star dust, expected to return to their prebirth nature as stars in the heavens, a destiny reserved for good philosophers and like-minded folks.

Furthermore, no one was expecting a final day of judgment. It has been suggested that Paul here is still using Stoic ideas since they believed in future judgment. This, however, is like comparing apples to oranges. Some Stoics believed that people who did evil would be judged in this life and would have suffering or a terrible death, or both, imposed upon them. Paul is not talking about this sort of temporal retribution. He is talking about a future judgment for all people on the day of the Lord, a day when all who have ever lived will need to give account to God for what they did with what they knew of him (cf. Rom 2). This end-time or eschatological judgment was not expected by anyone in Paul's audience. Many thought that the sun and earth were eternal and that things would just continue on as they had.

While some in Paul's audience might have agreed with most of what Paul said (but not what he meant), Acts 17:31 makes it clear that Paul did not simply use philosophical language to translate the gospel, or choose philosophical ideas and try to translate them into Christian statements. No, Paul here shows that all the ideas he has offered live outside of the worldviews of his audience. There is no way that any Stoic, Epicurean, Neo-Platonist or adherent to the traditional Greek pantheon of gods is going to accept the argument of Paul's speech in its entirety. Paul began his real argument in Acts 17:24-25 by asserting God's act of creating the cosmos. Paul then said that God made the world such that humans would seek him. Now he says that history not only had a starting point when it was created, but it has an ending point. No Greek philosophy had a place for a world that was first made by a deity and that would have its purpose completed on a coming day of judgment. Paul has told the Athenians the biblical story from creation to eschaton, from the beginning until the end. For his audience, time and history simply march along. They are without purpose in themselves and are not headed toward a specific endpoint. If there was any doubt that Paul was not actually espousing a Stoic view of reality, it would be gone now. It is this very story—one that moves from original creation to the new creation that began with Jesus' resurrection—that is the good news of what God has done in Jesus Christ.

Paul's assertion that God is going to judge the world in righteousness echoes a common scriptural tradition. Paul's words are virtually identical to those of the psalmists: "[God] himself will judge the inhabited world in righteousness" (Ps 9:8); and "[the LORD] is coming to judge the earth, to judge the inhabited world in righteousness" (Pss 96:13; 97:9). When Isaiah prophesies of a future Davidic ruler, he declares,

> He will not judge by what His eyes see,
> Nor make a decision by what His ears hear;
> But with righteousness He will judge the poor,
> And decide with fairness for the afflicted of the earth;
> And He will strike the earth with the rod of His mouth,
> And with the breath of His lips He will slay the wicked.
> Also righteousness will be the belt about His loins. (Is 11:3-5 NASB)

Isaiah also predicts future judgment on the peoples of the earth, saying,

> My righteousness is near, My salvation has gone forth,
> And My arms will judge the peoples. (Is 51:5 NASB)

We should not overlook the many biblical texts that declare that the Lord will judge his own people Israel, as though they can escape righteous judgment.[5] God declares through the prophet Joel,

> Let the nations be aroused
> And come up to the valley of Jehoshaphat,
> For there I will sit to judge
> All the surrounding nations. (Joel 3:12 NASB)

Micah declares that God will

> judge between many peoples
> And render decisions for mighty, distant nations.
> Then they will hammer their swords into plowshares
> And their spears into pruning hooks. (Mic 4:3 NASB)

At this point, Paul's words fit nothing his audience knows, but his words stand firmly within this biblical tradition. Even so, to validate his assertion, Paul, in good rhetorical manner, offers Jesus' resurrection, the *anastasis,* as the ultimate proof of Paul's claims. Paul started off with common cultural ground but uses that on his way to presenting a core piece of the gospel.

Here it should be noted that Paul does not simply instruct them to believe what he is saying, but he provides grounds for their belief. The resurrection of Jesus is critical here as elsewhere in Acts. Jesus' death would not have proved much to anyone except that, to Jews, this would mean that Jesus was accursed by God (cf. Deut 21:22, quoted by Paul in Gal 3:13). It was easy to find Jews who had been crucified by the Romans; so Jesus' crucifixion would have had no significance within the worldviews of Paul's audience.

On the other hand, resurrection had enormous consequences for his audience if this really happened. Back in 1985, some biblical scholars and others in various professions formed an organization called the Jesus Seminar. This group was created to destroy the historic Christian faith, and its founder, Robert Funk, was very explicit about this. At one point, the Jesus Seminar held a news conference with the Los Angeles County coroner, who stated that in her experience dead bodies stayed dead. This was supposed to prove that the resurrection of Jesus did not happen. This observation about dead bodies was hardly revolutionary.

In Paul's world, if a family member died, it was the duty of the other family members to prepare the body for burial and do the burying, generally on the same day the person died. There were no morticians or funeral homes to take care of all this messy, unpleasant business for you. Those who lived in the first century A.D. knew very well that when someone died, that person stayed dead. Consequently, when the first followers of Jesus declared that God had overruled the unjust condemnation of Jesus by raising him from the dead, it was a radical and highly questionable proclamation. Yet, this assertion is a key piece of the very first evangelistic speech by believers (cf. Acts 2:23-24). Paul himself states that this is an essential part of the gospel (1 Cor 15:1-8).

In Acts 17:31, Paul describes the resurrection in terms of those who saw Jesus alive after his death. Paul is presenting the resurrection of Jesus as a solid piece of evidence that what Paul says about God is true. He is telling his audience that in the middle of history an unexpected event has occurred.

Paul's emphasis upon eyewitnesses is important because in Paul's world being told something by an eyewitness carried far more weight than reading about it in some historical account, even if it was written by the eyewitness! Oral testimony was valued more highly. This requires of his audience that they not only rethink or change their minds about reality but that they look at evidence, something the Stoics and Epicureans could not produce for their own beliefs.

RESPONSES TO PAUL'S APPROACH

While chapter two briefly compared the response Paul received at Athens with that which he received in Lystra, more needs to be said. Paul's approach in content and style has held his audience's attention up until he says something unpalatable to all. Since the body was viewed by many to be a prison, as it was made from evil matter (and there is no good matter), returning to it after death was unthinkable. It is not surprising that some sneered at Paul when he made clear that *anastasis* was not a deity but a historical event, the resurrection of the body.

Since Plato's day, various philosophies and religions had taught that the body was something you would want to escape; so it is not surprising that Paul had three responses to his speech. Some mocked Paul for proclaiming the idea of the resurrection of the dead. Yet, Luke is quick to add that some took the approach of saying to Paul that they wanted to hear him again on this matter. Whether this was sincere or a polite way of ending the meeting is not clear, but it is better than being sneered at.

Finally, some joined Paul and believed (Acts 17:34). By God's grace, Paul's rhetorical style, content and logic led some of those present to change their minds about reality and to embrace a Jewish-Christian worldview as far as they understood it at that moment. Obviously, Paul would have to teach them more because they did not know about most of what Paul affirmed. This change, however, to accept the resurrection of the dead, was an enormous change. For accomplishing that, Paul gets high marks!

CONCLUSION

We have seen in Paul's speech to the Areopagus, philosophers and others present a model for (pre-)evangelism. Paul presents core biblical teachings, including the existence of the one true God; his providential activity both in creating the world and in continuing to provide life and breath and everything to its inhabitants; the foolishness of idols; the dignity of humans as created in the image of God; God's future judgment upon those who worship false deities; and the need to repent from these misguided religious beliefs and practices. While everything that Paul says is grounded in the Old Testament, he did not hesitate to present much of it with terminology familiar to the philosophers present. He also used the appropriate approach, classical rhetoric, which would be expected of someone who was truly educated.

Paul skillfully begins with a statement about the religiosity of his audience, but the philosophers present might have seen this as a critique of the religious beliefs and practices of most other people, and thus seen Paul as agreeing with them on this point. Paul makes several statements that the philosophers present, especially the Stoics, would have accepted. Paul demonstrated his knowledge of standard rhetorical techniques, especially in beginning his speech in a way designed to gain a hearing from Gentiles who knew nothing about the gospel except for what they had heard Paul proclaim in the marketplace. Paul cited one or more Greek poets as proofs for his argument and by doing this showed that he was not a babbler but an educated person whom the audience should regard positively. These quotations should be accepted as weighty evidence for the validity of Paul's argument. Paul built bridges where he could through his knowledge of the worldviews of his audience. Yet, he did not compromise the gospel.

Acts 17:24-31 is a brief summary of the biblical story from creation to consummation. So Paul's words might have been familiar to his audience, but he meant very different things by them. By utilizing them all within the divinely scripted story of God's work in the world as Creator, Sustainer and Judge, Paul made it abundantly clear that he was not simply repeating Stoic doctrine and appending Jesus' resurrection to the end of it. Paul chose a strategy that would help his audience go with him until he got to the decisive climax, in which he asserted that God would judge his audience by a man raised from the dead. Paul was not afraid to speak of the resurrection of Jesus, but he chose to put this one very controversial item at the end of his speech. Those who would have agreed with him up to that point would hopefully then also find Paul's statements about Jesus to be persuasive as well. Paul identified with his hearers.

Paul expressed core biblical ideas in culturally relevant ways. At the same time, Paul challenged his audience and offered them the solution to their ignorance and their futile pursuit of God through false religion. He even (most likely) began by complimenting his audience in their pursuit of the true God, finding something positive in their beliefs to begin his address to them. In all these ways, Paul demonstrated well what he later wrote to the Christians in Corinth regarding his conduct toward unbelievers. Paul stated,

> I became as a Jew to the Jews in order to gain the Jews, to those under the Law as under the Law, not being myself under the Law, in order to gain those under the Law, to those without the Law as one without the Law, not being without the Law of God but obedient to the law of Christ in order that I may gain those without the Law. I became weak to the weak in order that I may gain the weak. I have become all things to all people in order that by all means I may save some. And I do all things on account of the gospel. (1 Cor 9:20-23)

10

Going to Our Own Mars Hill

We have seen that Paul's message at Athens wasn't at all wrong-headed. Rather, it was an astutely contextualized presentation of the gospel. Paul masterfully wove together issues and concerns pertinent to both the Stoics and the Epicureans in his audience, all within a solidly Christian framework. Paul's speech was anchored in the Old Testament Scriptures, and he affirmed that the one true God is the Creator of all things, that idolatry is theologically misguided and that God's agent in the world is Christ the risen Lord, who calls for all without exception to repent.

What lessons does Paul's speech have to teach us about reaching our own Athens? At the beginning of the book we looked at some ways of doing so, including utilizing philosophical and scientific resources and arguments that spring from God's general revelation. And we built on this point in our discussion of natural theology in chapter seven. In addition to these points, here are a few considerations based on Paul's example.

DISTINGUISHING BETWEEN PERSONS AND BELIEFS

When Paul saw the idols in Athens, he was angered in his spirit. But did Paul lash out against the Athenians? No, Paul was very measured, respectful and gracious in his demeanor as he addressed them. He began by speaking of how remarkably religious Athens was, and he gave a respectful speech even though it involved a critique of Stoicism and Epicureanism as well as mention of the alien concept of resurrection. One lesson to learn here: Paul was able to distinguish between persons made in the image of God and the beliefs they held.

In our day of true-for-you-but-not-for-me relativism, many assume that if you don't accept their beliefs, you don't accept them.[1] Relativism collapses the two: if you reject the viewpoint of others, you are rejecting them personally. For the relativist, there is no graciously agreeing to disagree, which is the classical understanding of tolerance. But the relativistic view of tolerance (accepting all views as true) is not only incoherent and confused; it also creates unnecessary barriers to conversation.

Because all human beings are made in God's image, we can accept and befriend those whose beliefs differ from ours. There is no inherent contradiction between firmness of conviction and civil, gracious disagreement. Paul himself exhorted the Ephesians to "speak the truth in love" (Eph 4:15), and he exemplifies this exhortation in his speech to the Athenians.

DESCRIBING THE UNKNOWN GOD

The Athenian Areopagus would routinely hear advocates for particular deities present their cases in hopes that space would be provided for their gods or goddesses in the city's pantheon of divinities. Paul, however, did not present a new deity to the Athenians. Rather, he proclaimed a God already in their pantheon—the "unknown God"! Paul made an effort to build on what his audience already knew and embraced. Likewise, we too should look for ways to talk about the unknown God in contemporary culture.

Because many people in Western culture grow up exposed to the Christian faith to some degree, they will affirm that "something out there" accounts for the universe's existence and design. But they seem content with this detached deism that makes no personal demands on them. That is, whatever is "out there" is remote, and though this "something" wound up the universe, it has no real concern for the well-being of humanity. After all, look at the problem of evil and the wretched condition of our race. How could there be a caring God out there?

In response, we can affirm something quite remarkable about this "unknown God" in light of the universe he has created. After all, consider the staggering vastness of the universe that came about at the Big Bang, the vast energy contained within it that continues to spread out as the universe winds down, and the universe's remarkable precision tuning for human habitation. The psalmist (Psalm 8) and philosopher Immanuel Kant alike were stirred within and humbled when they gazed at the starry heavens above.

Figure 10.1. This altar (from the beginning of first century B.C.) was associated with the original walls of the city of Rome. The inscription is translated, "Whether to a God or Goddess sacred, C. Sestius (the son of Caius) Calvinus, praetor, by decree of the Senate restored (this)." This could have been the sort of altar dedicated to an "unknown god" Paul noticed in Athens. The inscription may be a ritual formula used to hide the name of the protecting divinity from enemies.

And the fact that people can recognize evil in the world suggests a moral compass that is not arbitrary. Kant spoke not only of the starry heavens above but also of "the moral law within." If real evils exist in the world—evils we associate with Stalin, Hitler, Pol Pot and Mao Tse-Tung—then we are assuming an objective design plan of sorts: there is a way things ought to be, and evil is a departure from that. But if there is no design plan and nature is all there is, then why think things should be any different from the way that they are? And maybe the evils in the world, especially when they directly affect us, can serve as something of a wake-up call for us. The familiar cry for justice—as old as humanity itself—suggests a transcendent moral standard above national laws and social contracts. Not only does evil remind us that things ought to be different from the way that they are; it also reminds us of the need for outside assistance to address profound evils both outside of us and within our own hearts. We all have a deep longing that evil will not have the last word.

What if, just maybe, there is some unknown God who, if only we reached out and searched for him, could be found? Maybe this unknown God—whose presence can be detected in the universe's beginning, vastness, energy and fine-tuning and in the moral awareness that we have—has actually done something more. Maybe this unknown God is less distant than we had thought. It would make sense that this unknown God could give greater clarity for us rather than leaving us with no guidance or hope at all. Maybe this God has taken the initiative to reveal and give hope in the midst of our miserable human condition. This was Paul's aim at Athens, to point to Christ as the unknown God's agent in the world to restore order, to offer forgiveness if we repent and to give us hope beyond the grave.

SIGNALS OF TRANSCENDENCE

Paul teaches us to utilize available indicators or signals of the transcendent. He speaks of people "groping" or "reaching for" God (Acts 17:27), although the verb form that Paul uses suggests that on their own they will fail, and hence the need for outside assistance. Paul points to one of the cultural touchstones of Athens to connect people to the gospel—namely, the altar to the "unknown God." He reinforces this by pagan utterances such as "by him we live and do what we do and exist" and "we are his offspring" (Acts 17:28).

Not only do intellectual and theological arguments matter, but so do certain practical considerations such as deep human needs and longings. Our experience is full of certain triggering conditions: the human quest for security and significance, the fear of death and the longing for immortality, the longing for justice, and the sense of awe and wonder.[2] These features of our existence leave us longing for something more. The novelist Elizabeth Gaskell wrote about a poor dying factory girl in her book *North and South:* "I think if this should be the end of all, and if all I have been born for is just to work my heart and life away in this [dreary] place. . . . I think, if this life is the end, and that there is no God to wipe away all tears from all eyes, I could go mad."[3]

In light of these profound longings, Jesus' own words reach to the very depths of our being. As the bread of life (Jn 6:35), he promises to satisfy our deepest hunger—a spiritual one. He promises to give "water of life" so that we will never thirst again (Jn 4:10; 7:38). He tells those who are weary and burdened, with guilt and shame and worry, that if they come to him, he will give them rest for their souls (Mt 11:28-30). Part of Jesus' mission was to grant his disciples the fullest life possible (Jn 10:10).

As C. S. Lewis argued, it would seem strange that we would have hunger or thirst if no food or water were around to satisfy it. Likewise, it would seem legitimate to consider our deepest inner needs as well. What if our deepest needs actually point to an ultimate source of satisfaction beyond any this-worldly existence?

Lewis wrote of "a desire for something that has never actually happened."[4] However enjoyable our earthly experiences are, we're never fully satisfied.

We yearn for something more, something beyond. As Lewis argued, we can't find transcendence and ultimacy in books or music:

> The books or the music in which we thought the beauty was located will betray us if we trust in them; it was not *in* them, it only came *through* them, and what came through them was longing. These things—the beauty, the memory of our own past—are good images of what we really desire; but if they are mistaken for the thing itself they turn into dumb idols, breaking the hearts of their worshippers.[5]

Our earthly enjoyments and awe-inspiring moments aren't ends in themselves. Our sense of wanting something more can point us to something no earthly thing can satisfy. These yearnings remind us of the previously cited statement from Augustine's *Confessions:* "You have made us for yourself, and our hearts are restless till they find their rest in you."[6]

EVANGELISM AND APOLOGETICS AS A PROCESS

Many of us think of evangelizing and defending the Christian faith primarily as an event rather than a process.[7] A one-size-fits-all approach may actually create barriers rather than build bridges; we should consider more carefully the most appropriate entry points for the gospel by better understanding our audience.

We have strongly emphasized how the speeches in Acts differ according to context. For example, Paul's speech to the Athenians was quite unlike Peter's at Pentecost. In Acts 2, Peter cited Scripture to religious Jews who considered it authoritative, and three thousand of them took the message to heart and became followers of Christ. By contrast, Paul's audience had no awareness of Scripture or its emphasis on monotheism, of creation out of nothing or of the emptiness of idolatry. In Athens, Paul was breaking new ground whereas Peter was reaping a harvest of theological seeds sown over the centuries through the Jews' exposure to God's special revelation through prophets and divine acts in history. Jesus expressed this point when he and his disciples were among the half-Jewish Samaritans:

> Do you not say, "There are yet four months, and then comes the harvest"? Behold, I say to you, lift up your eyes and look on the fields, that they are white for harvest. Already he who reaps is receiving wages and is gathering fruit for

life eternal; so that he who sows and he who reaps may rejoice together. For in this case the saying is true, "One sows and another reaps." I sent you to reap that for which you have not labored; others have labored and you have entered into their labor. (Jn 4:35-38 NASB)

In our day, the path from truth-denying secular postmodernism or an everything-goes New Age philosophy to an initial commitment to Christ involves many small steps and even exploratory side trails. Further, the path to becoming a mature believer who adeptly engages the contemporary mind one person at a time is many steps beyond that. Along this pilgrimage are many distinct points—from doubting truth to being uncomfortable with the contradictions within one's own worldview to trusting a believer to wanting to become like that believer and then embracing Christ. The progression could look something like that in table 10.1.

Table 10.1. Progressive Steps from Nonbelief to Mature Faith

-9	Suspicious of any truth claim or objective moral values—thoroughly secular, either postmodern or otherwise
-8	God is completely irrelevant to everything one values or to which one aspires
-7	Suspicion toward theism and the Christian faith in particular
-6	Engaging with believers; assuming that if the truth exists, it is not found in God
-5	Through believers, smug secularism challenged and shaken
-4	Thinking that the Christian faith is plausible, but still not believing it
-3	Desiring to be like the Christian(s) one has come to know
-2	Beginning to imagine oneself as a follower of Christ
-1	Seeing one's need for Christ
**	REPENTANCE AND FAITH IN CHRIST
1	Thinking and way of life still largely secular and postmodern, though committed to growing as a believer
2	Getting further involved in the community of believers
3	Realizing how life in Christ is to be lived out
4	Beginning to think biblically about relationships and issues of integrity
5	Growing in reliance on the Word and God's Spirit in daily life
6	Thinking more biblically about life, vocation, stewardship, use of spiritual gifts, communicating one's faith
7	Developing one's spiritual gifts, mentoring others, engaging the contemporary mind one person at a time

Typically, a brief conversation or sermon about Jesus will not dislodge disbelief. As with missionaries going to a crosscultural setting to reach people groups for Christ, God likewise exerts his power in our own settings through the common experiences of life—through conversations, relationships, education and reflection. Back in 1913, the Princeton theologian J. Gresham Machen observed that "God usually exerts that power in connection with certain prior conditions of the human mind, and it should be ours to create, so far as we can, with the help of God, those favorable conditions for the reception of the gospel."[8] He went on to say:

> False ideas are the greatest obstacles to the reception of the gospel. We may preach with all the fervor of a reformer and yet succeed only in winning a straggler here and there, if we permit the whole collective thought of the nation or of the world to be controlled by ideas which, by the resistless force of logic, prevent Christianity from being regarded as anything more than a harmless delusion.[9]

The need for having processing time to consider and then embrace Christ is evident when we contrast a naturalistic or secular mindset with a truly biblical outlook (see table 10.2).

Table 10.2. Contrast of Secular Outlook with Biblical Outlook

Worldview Category	Secular Outlook	Biblical Outlook
View of reality	Only the material world exists, and God does not. Humans are purely material beings. There is no afterlife, and miracles are impossible.	Both a material and a spiritual world exist. The relational, tri-personal God exists. There is an afterlife. Miracles are possible and do occur. Humans are spiritual beings, created to know and love God.
Origins	All that exists has been produced through mindless, impersonal, valueless material processes.	All reality besides God has been brought about by God's purposeful creation and design.
Humans	They are autonomous and free to chart their own course in life. On another view, humans are developed animals whose actions are determined by genes and environment.	They are made in God's image and with a God-given purpose. They are utterly dependent on God for their very existence and are accountable to him.
Morality	If objective moral values exist, they are not dependent upon God. Otherwise, morality tends to be seen as relative or cultural; each person or culture comes up with its own values. Morality is rooted in evolution and in human conventions, cultures and choices.	Morality is objective (for all people) and universally binding; its source is the character of God and his commands.
Authority	The individual human is not ultimately answerable to anyone except himself. He "creates" his own life's purpose and meaning.	God is the cosmic authority to whom every human must answer. He has designed humans for a particular purpose—to love him and love others.

Of course, every person's worldview or philosophy of life will reflect a religious-like heart commitment—either oriented toward the true God or to some idolatrous substitute. For our purposes, *secular* refers to a person on whom belief in God or Christ has no direct or conscious influence. If a person has been at home in a secular orientation for a long period of time, the Christian outlook will seem quite foreign. Mental and moral habits are so thoroughly embedded that the person will likely need more than a brief exposure to the gospel message. Any normal person will need time and relationship to process another worldview. We can be those who, through friendship and conversation, put a pebble in the spiritual shoes of our secular-minded friends to help them recognize inconsistencies in their philosophy of life and become uncomfortable with that way of thinking and then consider the Christian faith to be a viable alternative.[10]

Both evangelizing and defending the faith involve a process of engagement at various levels (social, intellectual, emotional, spiritual), and we enter into this process prayerfully and thoughtfully. And how we begin depends on where a person is—whether that person is suspicious of any truth-claims, acknowledges that God exists or is a Christian in name only. We should make it our prayer that, by God's grace, we can help a person move one step closer to becoming a disciple of Christ.

One way of encouraging this kind of exploration is a particular Meetup group (meetup.com) known as Socrates Café (socratescafemn.org). A group of thoughtful Christians in a church can start and lead such a philosophical discussion group in their community once a month, attracting thoughtful New Agers, atheists, skeptics, Hindus and Muslims. For a nominal cost, the Meetup website could be used to post meetings, topics and location on the Internet. The group discussion leader could (1) open a low-key discussion with the topic of the month, (2) go into a large-group interactive discussion with a lot of give and take, and then (3) wrap up the discussion and offer a personal perspective about the topic. After the group breaks up (and those who need to leave can do so), those who want to linger can (4) stay around for up to an hour to discuss the topic informally over coffee and treats.

What are some of the questions to be discussed? Here is a sampling: Can we know? What is really real? Do right and wrong exist? What happens at death? Does God exist? What is evil? Does history have a point? What is the meaning of life? Are miracles possible?[11] Or a church could use the same format but advertise—word of mouth is best—a regular open Q&A event, calling it, say, "seekers' forum" or "open forum."

Another forum could be a church hosting dinners (these could be at a restaurant). The table hosts invite the seeker and thinker, or perhaps simply international students at a nearby university, to hear a credible Christian speaker address important philosophical or scientific questions. Such meetings could be done in a home just as readily, though on a smaller scale. These are just some of the available resources that churches can utilize as they help modern-day Athenians take the next step to think about and hopefully discover the identity of the unknown God as revealed in Jesus of Nazareth.[12]

In addition to considering the process, Christians must dedicate themselves to building credibility and trust. Before Paul gave his speech at Athens, he embarked on his own fact-finding mission. We saw earlier that, just as biblical scholars study historical or cultural contexts and engage in word analysis to exegete (interpret or explain) a text, we too should exegete our own settings to better communicate the gospel to our culture and community. Although Paul was already well educated, he took the time to explore the particularities of Athens so that his message would be as contextualized and credible as possible. In following Paul's example, we contribute to an important first step for any communicator and defender of the gospel—building trust.

The campus ministry InterVarsity Christian Fellowship held a conference on how to communicate the gospel to postmoderns, those suspicious of truth claims and metanarratives, grand explanatory stories that claim to be universally true and applicable to every person.[13] As these campus workers discussed their experiences with postmoderns who came to Christ, a general consensus began to take shape. The first threshold for the postmodern to cross is a momentous one, moving from distrust to trust of Christians. If this credibility gap is not first addressed, the postmodern will in all likelihood not give the Christian message and messenger a serious chance. While we must be credible, caring, listening and loving to nonbelievers of all stripes, this seems to be especially necessary with postmoderns. We believers need to be a safe place for the skeptic and the truth denier.

Building credibility comes from being a good observer and listener. James reminds us to be "quick to listen" and "slow to speak" (Jas 1:19 NIV). Unfortunately, Christians seem to have a reputation for reversing these—being quick to speak and slow to listen. We are ready with answers before we know what a person's specific questions are. It's like the story of the pastor who gave the children's sermon on Easter Sunday. He asked the children gathered round him, "What is furry and has long ears and a cottontail and hops from one place to another?" One of the children replied, "I know the answer is Jesus, but it sure sounds like a rabbit to me." And while Jesus is indeed the ultimate answer to the world's problems, we often aren't very good at helping people connect the dots.

Yet as we take care to hear another's story, we earn the respect of the unbeliever and gain the privilege of being heard in return. We may find out all kinds of things—a bad experience with the church, misunderstandings about the Christian faith, a miserable father. In listening, without feeling the need to reply point for point, we treat the contemporary Athenian as a person, not a project. Once unbelievers can move from distrust to trust, then we can, with God's help, lead them across other thresholds: help arouse their curiosity, encourage openness to change in their lives and challenge them to move beyond meandering to seeking so that they might cross the threshold from darkness into the light of God's kingdom.

CHALLENGING THE IDOLATRIES OF OUR DAY

Some critics have claimed that early Christians attempted to mimic surrounding pagan ideas to make the gospel more culturally and religiously palatable to pagans. So Jesus, they claim, is simply another mythical hero with an unusual birth who joined the pantheon of other dying-and-rising gods in the Mediterranean world at that time. Ironically, this previously discredited view, though once dead, has risen again in various places, including the movie *Zeitgeist*.[14] In the monotheistic Judaic culture of first-century Palestine, which was resistant to pagan ideas, there just were no dying-and-rising-god cults; also, any apparent parallels actually date to the second century A.D., making this pagan-influence idea all the more implausible.[15]

Knowing the strong Jewish opposition to idolatry and pagan influences, Paul was certainly not one to be taken in by non-Jewish, pagan ideas. Furthermore, though he was tactful and gracious toward the Athenians, Paul wasn't afraid to challenge idolatry and false, destructive theologies. Though

Paul was a bridge builder, he wasn't a compromiser.

This is evident in at least three ways. First, to mention Jesus' bodily resurrection to Platonized Greeks did not win him any sympathy points, but Paul was more concerned about truth than fitting in with cultural norms and generally accepted beliefs. When in Athens, he didn't do as the Athenians did. However, Paul sought to be culturally relevant. Second, Paul pointed out theological shortcomings of Athenian idolatry and polytheism. Paul was intensely committed to monotheism, and, as we saw in chapters six and nine, he drew on the anti-idol polemic against Babylon's gods in Isaiah 40–55.[16] Third, he affirmed that Jesus the Messiah—not Caesar—is God's agent in the world and that God will bring about his judgment and righteous rule through Jesus Christ, whom he raised from the dead. Paul referred to Jesus using terms such as *Lord, Son of God, King* and *Savior,* terms that had strong anti-imperial connotations in his day. Whether at Athens or Corinth, Paul opposed any idea or philosophy that exalted itself against the knowledge of the Messiah (2 Cor 10:5).

Ultimately, idolatry is the turning of God's good gifts into God substitutes, that is, making good things into ultimate things. These gifts include human creativity, intelligence and rationality, material wealth, beauty, human government to maintain order, culture—all of which can become idols. As followers of King Jesus, we are called to resist and challenge in word and deed the idolatries and antikingdom ideologies of our day.

We are well aware that the hallowed halls of the academy are not typically characterized by humility and generosity of spirit. More common are pride, posturing, power-playing, politics and political correctness, a false tolerance that is polite toward those who agree but angry and even hostile toward those who disagree. Many fragile egos can be found within the ivory tower!

What's more, behind many of the academy's intellectual exertions are all manner of idolatries. After all, idolatries are often embedded in and masked by one's worldview or philosophy of life. Worldviews are not merely intellectual in nature. Rather, one's beliefs and attitudes reflect a heart commitment, which is at the core of any worldview. Not surprisingly, many in the academy oppose the idea of a good and just God because of his status as the cosmic authority. After all, this status presents a threat to our own absolute autonomy as human beings. If such a God exists, this changes everything. The atheist philosopher Thomas Nagel candidly admitted: "I hope there is no God! I don't want there to be a God; I don't want a universe to be like that."[17] He adds that a "cosmic authority problem" governs much of academia.[18]

One prominent idol in our culture, and in many others, is sexual freedom. If a person's idol is sexual freedom, he can come up with all kinds of rationalizations to justify it. The agnostic thinker Aldous Huxley once wrote that he and his intellectual peers objected to morality because it interfered with their quest for sexual liberation; thus, he frankly admitted, they were able to come up with rationalizations to justify their lifestyle.[19]

What are some other idolatries in our day?

- *Political:* trusting in a political party or candidate to deliver a nation or in the government to provide for us from womb to tomb so as to remove all obstacles to personal security—or perhaps grasping political power for self-serving ends rather than bringing benefit for the common good

- *Economic:* relying on financial security; lacking contentment; envying those who are wealthier and not caring for people in genuine need

- *Philosophical/religious:* trusting in human-made systems of thought, including an impersonal ultimate reality (Brahman, the *dharma,* the Tao), stringent legalisms, gnostic spiritualities, reductionistic naturalism, or karmic beliefs, all of which ultimately diminish human dignity, reduce human flourishing and further alienate us from relationship with the one true God

- *Technological:* trusting in automation, technique and convenience so that God seems increasingly distant and unnecessary to our everyday lives, prayer and faith are seemingly irrelevant, and we easily become practical atheists

- *Relational:* placing all our hopes in relationships or romances to bring us security and significance

How do we challenge the idolatry in our contemporary setting? Consider the area of relationships. Pastor Tim Keller advises Christians not to simply "scold" relativists for inferior moral standards or mushy views of truth. Premarital sex and sexual lust, say, are wrong, but these "bad things" are symptoms of something deeper:

Instead of telling them they are sinning because they are sleeping with their girlfriends or boyfriends, I tell them that they are sinning because they are looking to their romances to give their lives meaning, to justify and save them, to give them what they should be looking for from God. This idolatry leads to anxiety, obsessiveness, envy, and resentment. I have found that when you describe their lives in terms of idolatry, postmodern people do not give much resistance. Then Christ and his salvation can be presented not (at this point) so much as their only hope for forgiveness, but as their only hope for freedom.[20]

Or consider technology, which tends to create a depersonalized existence. Deep, personal relationships are squeezed out of our lives by encroaching technology. Face-to-face conversations are replaced by Facebook and Internet surfing, conversations interrupted by a steady stream of cell-phone calls and text messages, and family mealtimes replaced by screens of one sort or another. Technology itself is not the problem, but we can easily let it rule our lives. Technology, modern conveniences and the creation of virtual realities through video games and constant movie watching make it possible to imagine our world in such a way that we ignore the actual reality of God's gracious presence within it. We can easily come to love a world that is "passing away" (1 Jn 2:17), a falsely structured "reality" that diminishes personal relationships and Christian discipleship.[21]

Though the apostle Paul did not address depersonalizing technology, he was dealing with many depersonalized versions of the ultimate reality. In certain strands of Greek philosophical thought in his day and beyond, God or the Ultimate was static (the eternal forms), detached (the Absolute), impersonal (Fate), unmoved (impassible) principle. God was not the deeply personal agent of Scripture, who exerts his will and power by bringing the universe from nothing, can even be moved by human sin and suffering, and acts redemptively in that world. In many Eastern views, the ultimate reality (Brahman, the *dharma*) may be an impersonal, pure, unified consciousness or law.

The Christian response must be to recover personhood, beginning with our conception of the triune God (theology). We must not think of or proclaim God as detached and removed from human events and evil, but as the tri-personal, intrinsically relational God who is active in the world. And if our view of God is impersonal and detached, then our view of humanity (anthropology) will be depersonalized, and the value of the individual will be lowered, sometimes to the point of insignificance, as within many strands of Hinduism.[22] And if nature is the ultimate reality, humans are likewise commonly reduced to the status of animals.

JESUS: THE CLIMAX OF HISTORY AND THE FULFILLMENT OF OUR HIGHEST IDEALS

Paul closes his Areopagus speech by referring to Jesus as God's appointed agent in the world, whom he raised from the dead (Acts 17:31). Paul emphasizes the historical, risen Jesus as the climactic revelation of the one true God. In the early church, and even in some places in the New Testament, Christians would emphasize how Jesus fulfills not only the Old Testament but also the best ideas in human philosophies and the deepest human longings and ideals expressed in ancient literature and stories. These noble ideas and heroic characters were foreshadowings, anticipations of something greater. As C. S. Lewis rightly observed, Jesus, the Word who became flesh and lived among us (Jn 1:14), is "myth became fact."[23] Jesus as the ultimate human, the second Adam, both epitomizes and embodies the loftiest of human aspirations and the best of human wisdom and virtue across the ages.

According to the author of Hebrews, Jesus identified with us in our suffering and was tempted in every way that we are, but was without sin (Heb 2:18; 4:15). Yet the author of Hebrews also emphasizes that because of Jesus' identification with human beings and his agonizing crucifixion on their behalf, he becomes the "champion" or "hero" (*archēgos*) who secures our salvation (Heb 2:10; 12:2). This same term was used by Euripides of the divine hero Hercules, who wrestled with and conquered Death (Thanatos) and rescued Alcestis, his deceased wife.[24]

Beyond the text of the New Testament, the earliest Christians utilized the writings of pagan classical literature to support Christian belief.[25] They attempted to show that the Christian faith was not some recent innovation but was rooted in antiquity. God spoke through Moses about creation, and some early church fathers claimed, though incorrectly, that Plato's certain references to creation in his *Timaeus* were taken from Genesis. Justin Martyr sought to show that the Logos (Word/Reason) in Jesus was revealed in wise pagans before Jesus came, claiming that Christ had been "known in part even by Socrates."[26]

In fact, in the writings of early Christian apologists, Christ was frequently compared to Socrates. The Ten Commandments were seen as a valuable summary of God's law, both natural and revealed. Justin wrote in his *Second Apology,* "Whatever things were rightly said among all men are the property of us Christians." Two of the most important sources used by Christians were Virgil's *Fourth Eclogue* (written 41 or 40 B.C.) and the *Sibylline Oracles.* Virgil prophesied a golden age in which a virgin would bear new offspring of divine origin: "The last age . . . is born anew . . . : now from high heaven a new generation comes down. Yet do thou at that boy's birth, in whom the iron race shall begin to cease, and the golden to arise over all the world. . . . He shall . . . rule the world." This, Augustine believed, referred to Christ. Also, the *Sibylline Oracles* (second century B.C.) were given by the Sibyl, the prophetess among the Greeks who predicted the eventual destruction of the world; some of Christianity's earliest defenders claimed that this was a theme found in their Scriptures as well.

Further, another church father, Clement of Alexandria, believed that Odysseus, the hero of Homer's *Odyssey,* was a picture of Christ. While his men stopped their ears, Odysseus was tied to the mast of a ship while listening in agony to the alluring songs of the Sirens, ultimately triumphing over them. Likewise, Jesus was fastened to a cross to bear the agony of sin and exile that humans deserved, yet was victorious in the end. This Homeric story, like many others in Greco-Roman literature, was viewed by the earliest Christians as a foreshadowing of the Christ and anticipatory of the One who appeared in history to bring them to completion in history.

The fourth-century church historian Eusebius attempted to show that the Christian faith and Christ himself were anchored in antiquity and that Christian history was a universal history. According to the eminent church historian Jaroslav Pelikan, "Antiquity was widely regarded in pagan thought as lending authority to a system of thought or belief," and Christians sought to show the superiority of the Christian faith over pagan philosophies and ideals.[27] Moses and the prophets, it was maintained, were earlier than Plato and Homer.

Not all, however, agreed with this "argument from antiquity"—Ambrose of Milan, for example. Yet the earliest Christians are to be credited for their attempt to build bridges with pagan culture as they mined Greek and Roman literature and history to connect the gospel to their audience.

What about building such bridges today? Consider world religions. It is not unusual for Hindus to disregard questions about the historicity of Jesus. For them, the beauty and truth of the Sermon on the Mount are what matter most. Likewise, devotees of the Hindu god Krishna, an avatar of the god Vishnu, are unconcerned about whether he existed in history. Historicity is irrelevant. Rather, the inspiring stories of Krishna are important. We can ask, however, What if divine wisdom and virtue stepped into history and became human? And what if this historical personage rose from the dead to vindicate his authoritative claims? Surely, these are no trivial questions!

Lord of the Rings author J. R. R. Tolkien made this very point. A master of fantasy and myth himself, he observed that the Gospels contain "all the essence of fairy-stories," but this story has actually entered into history. Indeed, Legend and History come together in Jesus of Nazareth. This "fairy story" has the "inner consistency of reality." It becomes true without losing its deeper cosmic significance. This story begins with joy—and ends with it—and it is the most exalted kind of joy. To reject it leads either to sadness or to wrath. The gospel, Tolkien affirms, "has not abrogated legends; it has hallowed them, especially the 'happy ending.'"[28]

As with the earliest Christians, we in our own Athens today should emphasize how redemptive stories in movies, wisdom in philosophy, virtues in the world's religions and mythical stories promising life happily ever after all find their real fulfillment and realization in our Lord and Savior Jesus Christ, "in whom are hidden all the treasures of wisdom and knowledge" (Col 2:3 NASB). It is this Jesus whom we are to proclaim in the marketplace of ideas, the One who is the source and embodiment of truth, beauty and goodness.

CONCLUDING REMARKS

Paul's speech at Athens offers us a rich resource as we speak to contemporary Athenians. Rather than a bungled, but later abandoned, scheme to build bridges with pagans, Paul's gospel-centered, contextualized speech serves as a wise guide for Christian witness in the present.

We have reviewed the historical, cultural, philosophical and religious context of Athens, and we have examined Paul's speech in light of the Hebrew Scriptures and the reality of Jesus the Messiah as the fulfillment of

God's special revelation and the climactic outworking of his purposes in history.

Drawing on Paul's speech, we have explored a few avenues of application for a contemporary setting. We urge our readers to extend these lines of thinking and their applications into similar settings, as well as to open new lines of exploration relevant to their context and situation. It is our prayer that God will use this book in the lives of many Christians to help connect modern-day Athenians to the good news of the gospel and to uphold its integrity and credibility in the marketplace of ideas.

Resources for Further Reading

Books on the Christian Worldview

Bartholomew, Craig G., and Michael W. Goheen. *Christian Philosophy: A Systematic and Narrative Introduction*. Grand Rapids: Baker Academic, 2013. This traces philosophical thought from ancient Greece to postmodern times, engaging with it in the context of the Christian metanarrative and worldview.

Goheen, Michael W., and Craig G. Bartholomew. *Living at the Crossroads: An Introduction to the Christian Worldview*. Grand Rapids: Baker Academic, 2008. One of the best introductions to the Christian worldview available. Thoughtfully reviews the biblical story (metanarrative) with excellent historical background and insightful application to various disciplines.

Naugle, David. *Philosophy: A Student's Guide*. Nashville: B & H Academic, 2012. A handy guide to a Christian perspective on metaphysics (reality), anthropology (humankind), epistemology (knowledge), ethics, aesthetics and the vocation of Christian philosophers.

———. *Worldview: The History of a Concept*. Grand Rapids: Eerdmans, 2002. A more detailed overview of the worldview concept in philosophy and its use in Protestantism, Catholicism and Eastern Orthodoxy. A strong emphasis on worldview as a heart commitment, not simply an intellectual grid.

Plantinga, Cornelius, Jr. *Engaging God's World: A Christian Vision of Faith, Learning, and Living*. Grand Rapids: Eerdmans, 2002. A basic introduction to the Christian worldview of creation, fall and redemption—with a view to the relevance of the Christian worldview in higher education and vocation.

Evangelism and Apologetics Resources

Copan, Paul. *"How Do You Know You're Not Wrong?"*: *Responding to Objections That Leave Christians Speechless*. Grand Rapids: Baker Books, 2005. Deals with a range of questions such as the problem of skepticism, the soul and the brain, animal rights issues, naturalism versus theism, proving every belief scientifically, the biblical canon, and the Gnostic Gospels.

———. *Is God a Moral Monster? Making Sense of the Old Testament God.* Grand Rapids: Baker Books, 2011. An accessible book on Old Testament ethical challenges about slavery, the killing of the Canaanites, harsh punishments, kosher laws, God's jealousy and God's command to Abraham to kill Isaac.

———. *Loving Wisdom: Christian Philosophy of Religion.* St. Louis: Chalice Press, 2007. An introduction to themes in the philosophy of religion, structured around the Christian story of the triune God, creation, fall, redemption and re-creation. This book deals with the coherence of God's attributes, the problem of evil, arguments for God's existence, the logical consistency of the doctrines of the Trinity, incarnation and atonement.

———. *"That's Just Your Interpretation": Responding to Skeptics Who Challenge Your Faith.* Grand Rapids: Baker Books, 2001. A guide to understanding issues about Genesis and science, reincarnation, divine foreknowledge and human freedom, predestination, the reliability of the Gospels, the question "If God made the universe, who made God?" and much more.

———. *"True for You, but Not for Me": Overcoming Common Objections to Christian Faith.* Minneapolis: Bethany House, 2009. An overview and response to questions related to relativism, religious pluralism, the uniqueness of Christ and those who have never heard of Jesus.

———. *When God Goes to Starbucks: A Guide to Everyday Apologetics.* Grand Rapids: Baker Books, 2008. This book deals with questions about homosexuality, being born gay and gay marriage; Jesus' alleged mistakenness about his return; the imprecatory psalms; warfare in the Old Testament; whether God can make a stone so big that he can't lift it; miracles; whether God is arrogant and narcissistic; and the problem of differing Christian denominations.

Copan, Paul, and Matthew Flannagan. *Did God Really Command Genocide? Coming to Terms with the Justice of God.* Grand Rapids: Baker Books, 2014. An expansion on the morality of warfare in the Old Testament in ethical, philosophical, theological and biblical perspective.

Copan, Paul, and Robertson McQuilkin. *Introduction to Biblical Ethics.* 3rd ed. Downers Grove, IL: InterVarsity Press, 2014. An extensive, nontechnical guide and overview of ethical themes that follows the Scriptures as closely as possible. The book includes discussions of love, law, sin, virtues and vices—as well as euthanasia, abortion, bioethics, just war and pacifism, church and

state issues, the Christian home, and much more. The book includes relevant
illustrations and applications.

Craig, William Lane. *Hard Questions, Real Answers*. Wheaton, IL: Crossway, 2007.
This book addresses challenging questions at a very accessible level, dealing with
doubt, unanswered prayer and failure as well as thinking about homosexuality,
abortion, hell, the uniqueness of Christ and the question of the unevangelized; it
also emphasizes the importance of the life of the mind.

———. *On Guard: Defending Your Faith with Reason and Precision*. Colorado
Springs: David C. Cook, 2010. An entry-level guide to apologetics, including
arguments for God's existence and for Jesus' resurrection and discussion of the
problem of evil and the meaning of life without God. For a more intermediate
discussion of apologetics, see William Lane Craig's *Reasonable Faith*, 3rd ed.
(Wheaton, IL: Crossway, 2008).

Craig, William Lane, and Paul M. Gould, eds. *The Two Tasks of the Christian Scholar:
Redeeming the Soul, Redeeming the Mind*. Wheaton, IL: Crossway, 2007. This
book emphasizes how Christian scholarship can impact the academy, which can
in turn have a wide-ranging impact on the broader culture. Both mind and soul
need to be affected by the gospel, and the academy yields a significant influence
that should not be ignored by the church.

Koukl, Greg. *Tactics: A Game Plan for Discussing Your Christian Convictions*. Grand
Rapids: Zondervan, 2009. A wise guide for going deeper in conversation about
the Christian faith, with much valuable material about probing faulty assumptions and misleading terminology.

Moreland, J. P. *The God Conversation: Using Stories and Illustrations to Explain Your
Faith*. Downers Grove, IL: InterVarsity Press, 2007. A guide to explaining the
gospel and defending the faith using practical illustrations and stories.

———. *Kingdom Triangle*. Grand Rapids: Zondervan, 2009. A resource that emphasizes the importance of the life of the mind in thinking Christianly and of spiritual disciplines in the formation of Christlike practice and the miraculous power
of the Spirit.

———. *Love Your God with All Your Mind*. Colorado Springs: NavPress, 2007. An
extensive discussion on using our minds for God's glory and the importance of
thinking Christianly.

Newman, Randy. *Corner Conversations: Engaging Dialogues About God and Life*.
Grand Rapids: Kregel, 2006. Takes *Questioning Evangelism* a step further in discussing sex, homosexuality, life after death and the uniqueness of Jesus.

———. *Questioning Evangelism: Engaging People's Hearts the Way Jesus Did*. Grand

Rapids: Kregel, 2004. A book that advocates and exemplifies a superb engaging style of "dialoguing" the gospel—responding to the critic's questions with questions of your own to go deeper in discussions on homosexuality, tolerance, hypocrisy, hell and AIDS.

Wright, N. T. *The Resurrection of the Son of God*. Minneapolis: Fortress, 2003. The historicity, nature and significance of Jesus' bodily resurrection are at the heart of the gospel. This book is the best for describing competing views in the first century A.D. and objections today. It is not strictly a book on a Christian worldview, but without the resurrection of Jesus there is no valid Christian worldview.

DISCUSSION QUESTIONS

Chapter 1: Welcome to Athens

1. Read Acts 17 in its entirety.

2. Afterwards, discuss the context of Paul's situation in Athens. What has led him to Athens in the first place?

3. What are your initial impressions of Paul's situation at Athens?

4. What are your initial impressions of Paul's speech at Athens?

5. As you have read this chapter, what do you hope to gain from a study of Paul's speech at Athens?

6. In what ways do you think Paul's speech connects to your present situation and relationships?

Chapter 2: Was Paul's Speech at Athens a Mistake?

1. Had it ever occurred to you that Paul was wrong-headed in his methodology at Athens?

2. When you read that some scholars have thought this, what was your reaction? Do their arguments seem to have validity?

3. Have you come across Christians who oppose any study of philosophy or apologetics? What arguments or reasons do they give? How do you respond to them?

4. How does the book of Acts emphasize the life of the mind and the importance of thinking? How does the rest of the New Testament emphasize these things?

5. Read the account of Paul's visit (with Barnabas) to Lystra in Acts 14:1-18.

Compare his speech at Lystra (Acts 14:15-17) to the speech at Athens (Acts 17:24-31). In what ways is Paul's method the same? What other features of his Lystra speech stand out to you?

6. Read 1 Corinthians 9:19-27. From what you know of Paul, how does he contextualize his message for Greeks and for Jews?

7. In what you have read so far, how does Paul's approach help us as we seek to proclaim and defend the gospel in different contexts?

Chapter 3: Paul's Athens

1. Read Acts 14:1-20. Compare the cultural, religious and philosophical elements of Lystra to those of Athens. Why was the speech given in Acts 17:22-31 not also used in Lystra?

2. Thinking of the question above about Lystra, what do Paul's approach in Lystra and his approach at Athens illustrate about Paul as an evangelist?

3. Generally speaking, in Paul's world, a philosophy was primarily a set of beliefs that led to a particular way of living. Religion, on the other hand, was primarily a set of rituals that one performed, without there necessarily being any principles or rules or guidance for daily living in them. What does the message that Paul brought to Athens look more like, a philosophy or a religion? Why?

4. What might the average Athenian—slave, shopkeeper, day laborer and so forth—who did not have time or leisure to be a philosopher, have believed? A specific philosophy? A specific religion? A syncretistic mix of all?

5. How much reflection on the possible falseness of one's religion or philosophy were the socially elite Athenians likely to carry out? The average, non-elite Athenians?

6. Except for the Epicureans and Stoics whom Paul encountered, how well could an Athenian articulate the nature of his or her religion or philosophy and provide arguments for it or against other possible views?

Chapter 4: Our Athens

1. How would any of these ancient Athenians compare to modern

Athenians in thinking through their worldviews and being able to defend them and critique other views?

2. What do you consider to be important philosophical or moral issues that Christians need to be able to address? In your estimation, what does our Athens look like?

3. What bridges have you used in the past to help connect people to "the unknown God"?

4. Have you gotten any new bridge-building ideas through this study? Science? News stories related to the problem of evil? Crisis points in your friends' lives?

5. Philosophy and science can be important disciplines to open doors of conversation with unbelievers. What other disciplines or areas of study can help build bridges for the gospel?

6. What do you think about Luke's strategy in comparing Paul to Socrates? Is this instructive in any way?

7. What are your impressions of table 4.2, comparing theism and naturalism? Do you find this helpful in any way?

8. In what ways do you find the examples of Justin Martyr and Augustine important as we go to our Athens today?

9. What did you think of the historical arguments for Jesus' resurrection? Are there any other arguments you have heard in support of the historicity of the resurrection?

10. Describe conversations you have had with people who consider themselves relativists.

11. Have you encountered any expressions of anti-rational emotivism? Besides those covered in the book, what types of emotivism do you consider prevalent in our culture?

12. Have you encountered syncretism and religious pluralism? How would you describe these encounters?

13. Why do you think religious pluralism appeals to so many people? What are some responses to pluralism that come to mind?

14. How are science and scientism different? Why is it important to distinguish between these two? Why is scientism misguided?

Chapter 5: Paul's Speeches in Acts

1. Before reading this chapter, what type (genre) of literature did you think Acts was?

2. What purpose/purposes do you think Luke had in writing Acts? Why do you think this?

3. In modern post-Enlightenment Western cultures, history is often viewed as a scientific task that seeks to describe the past exactly as it happened, with no motive for recounting the past except for knowledge of what happened "back then." Why is this impossible?

4. Given the fact that no one can talk or write about the past without it being a selective account told from a specific perspective or social location, how do you evaluate Luke's efforts to teach believers how to approach evangelism or other matters for disciples, rather than simply telling the facts?

5. Think of stories that you have read or watched or heard besides those in the Bible. What principles or ideas do any of these narratives teach? Are these narratives of fictional or actual events?

6. What is the value or authority of any of these principles from stories that are fictional? What principles are communicated by accounts of actual events?

7. As an experiment, think of an important event in your own life. Try to tell someone else about this event with your only purpose being to entertain the other person. Now tell the same story with the intent of teaching some idea or principle to the other person. How do your two accounts of the same event differ based upon your goal in each narrative?

8. How might it change the way you think about the contents of Acts to view it as the second volume of the two-volume work Luke-Acts, seeing Luke 1:1-4 as the introduction for the book of Acts?

9. Acts shows evangelism in varying contexts. Read Acts 14:8-20 and 17:16-34. How do the contexts of these two events differ? How does

Paul's speech in Lystra compare to Paul's speech in Athens? How would you explain the differences?

10. Read all of Acts 16–17. How does Acts present Paul's missionary work in terms of success? How do you think that Luke/Paul would have defined *success*?

11. What do you think was important for Paul as he looked back at his experience in Athens and recounted it to Luke?

Chapter 6: Paul's Audience

1. Luke teaches his audience how to proclaim the gospel through models in Acts. How do you evaluate this approach? How could Luke have been more or less effective in making points along the way through Acts to be sure that his audience understood what he wanted them to understand? What does Luke's approach tell you about the Christians for whom Luke wrote Acts?

2. Having learned more about Paul's environment and audience, how well do you think his audience would have responded to well-known approaches to preaching the gospel today? Paul clearly had some obstacles to overcome. What are those obstacles that shaped his approach?

3. What obstacles to evangelism do we face today? In what ways might the core issues that confronted Paul be similar to the issues we confront today, even if the historical details are very different between then and now?

4. How much do you know about the worldviews of people you come into contact with daily?

5. If you wanted to learn more about what your audience thinks, what their worldviews are, how would you go about this?

6. How much effort do you think should be put into reading or listening to non-Christian material in order to be able to understand your audience?

7. Some Christians might say that it is a compromise of your faith to read what nonbelievers have written about worldview or that it might weaken your faith. What is your perspective?

8. If you were concerned that reading about other worldviews might challenge your faith, how could you address that concern?

9. Paul's speech focused heavily upon the intellectually oriented viewpoints of his audience. How much of the challenge of reaching your Athenian audience is a matter of intellectual understanding, and how much is it other issues? What are those other issues?

10. What did Luke's audience need to know to be competent readers, able to understand what Acts seeks to convey?

11. Think of yourself as being in the situation of Luke's audience. There is only the Old Testament for Scripture, plus some teaching from a traveling evangelist or a letter by Paul or other writers. There are no Christian books, Christian bookstores, or Christian radio or television programs, and the only church that you know is the group of ten to twenty people who meet each Sunday in someone's home. How do you learn more about what it means to live as a disciple of Jesus? If the only New Testament book you had were Acts, what would you do?

Chapter 7: Paul's Gospel for the Educated

1. Describe what you have heard or read outside the Bible about the contents of the gospel. How does this compare with Paul's statement of the gospel?

2. Paul treats Jesus' resurrection as all-important, yet in our day many Christians think little about the meaning or consequences of the resurrection of Jesus. Why do you think that this is so?

3. What would Paul have us proclaim about Jesus' resurrection?

4. How has your view of God changed from before your conversion until now? What can you say about God—without using big theological words like *omnipresent* or *omnipotent*? Why is this an important question?

5. Which belief of Paul's do you think that Christians today embrace the most? Which one do they discuss or believe the least? How might the answer to this question be based upon the culture in which we live?

6. Paul's theology is firmly rooted in the Old Testament and (Christian) Jewish interpretation of Scripture, yet many Christians know little if anything about the Old Testament. Why is this? How might this be remedied?

7. What does the Old Testament teach about God beyond his existence?

8. How do you think the Old Testament presentation of God compares to how the New Testament presents God?

9. What do you think that most non-Christians around you believe about G/god?

10. What do you think that most Christians around you believe about God?

11. Paul believed in the grand story presented in Scripture of God's unfolding plan for the cosmos and humans in particular. How would you tell this grand story in today's language so that it would be meaningful to Christians and non-Christians alike?

12. Paul preached about God's grace in Christ. He also preached about a coming judgment upon people for how they responded to the light that they had in seeking or not seeking God. Many in our culture today reject the idea of a future judgment. Why do you think this is so? How might you address this subject with someone who does not accept that God would judge anyone?

Chapter 8: The Art of Persuasion

1. In what ways do people in our culture argue for positions? How is it similar to and different from the Greco-Roman rhetorical approach?

2. Some urge that Christians should stop arguing about doctrine, if not ditch doctrine completely. What do you think Paul would say about this move?

3. What ideas or quotations from various authoritative or culturally familiar sources in our day provide material that might be usable in the same way that Paul used ideas and quotations from his cultural context?

4. How can you distinguish between biblical truths presented with terminology from our culture and biblical truths that have been replaced with elements of the culture? How do you determine if some idea or teaching compromises the gospel?

5. Some would object to using persuasive techniques, such as Paul's use of established rhetorical practices for persuasive speeches. What do you think?

6. How does crafting a message about the gospel in ways that are deliberately chosen to persuade others affect the content of the message?

7. What place does philosophy have in explaining or understanding the Christian faith? Why?

8. In following the conventions of Greco-Roman rhetoric, Paul essentially played by the rules of his culture. Would this be a good or bad idea in our setting? How do we differentiate between appropriate means of persuasion and inappropriate ones?

9. Read Philippians 3:1-14 and Acts 21:39–22:16 and 22:22-29. Thinking about these verses and Paul's experiences as described in Acts, what aspects of his education, upbringing and experiences prepared Paul for speaking to the Athenians?

10. What aspects of your education, upbringing and experiences could contribute to your ability to present the truths of the gospel and the biblical story?

11. How comfortable are you with explaining the meaning of the gospel and the larger story of God's actions in the world, particularly through his agent, Jesus of Nazareth? Why?

12. Read Acts 14:1-20. How does Paul's theological presentation differ from his presentation to a different group of Gentiles at Lystra?

Chapter 9: Acting on the Truth

1. Paul focuses his exhortation to the Athenians on their need to repent and depart from idolatry. He could have talked about many other sins, such as sexual immorality, but does not. What does this suggest about what Paul did stress?

2. One rarely hears the word *repent* among Christians in the West anymore. Why do you think this is so? How can this word be restored to Christian preaching? What are the challenges to preaching repentance?

3. It appears from the speech itself that this is the first time that Paul has spoken to these people and he is calling for repentance from idolatry and faith in the true God right then and there. What do you think might have been going through the minds of Paul's Athenian audience during this

encounter? If you think this would be effective in your context, what essential points would you cover? How might you tie the gospel into the language of your audience?

4. What does the larger context of the speech, Acts 17:16-21, tell you about Paul's previous action in relation to his speech?

5. Some would say that when the gospel is preached, there should always be an invitation of some sort to commit one's life to Jesus. What do you think? What might be a context in which an invitation would be appropriate? What would be a context in which an invitation would not be appropriate?

6. What would a call for repentance have meant for an Athenian in Paul's day? What would it mean for a modern Athenian?

7. Looking at all of Paul's speech, what is Paul essentially asking the Athenians to do in giving up idols and seeking the "unknown God"?

8. What are your observations on the benefits of philosophy in the lives of Justin Martyr and Augustine?

9. There are many professing Christians who would say that Jesus and his followers never went to school or were trained in understanding Scripture or other worldviews. Why might that be invalid or irrelevant to believers today?

10. How would you respond to someone who advocates Christian anti-intellectualism because the Bible tells you all that you need to know about God?

Chapter 10: Going to Our Own Mars Hill

1. In what ways has this study of Acts 17 alerted you to building bridges with a non-Christian friend or conversation partner?

2. In past conversations, have you experienced the need to distinguish between the person and the beliefs that person holds? Tell about this dynamic. How is Paul's example helpful here?

3. How can the "unknown God" idea from Athens open doors for discussion in our own friendships and circles of influence? The book touched on the problem of evil and the quest for justice in this regard. What are some other possibilities?

4. This chapter touches on arguments from transcendence. What are your impressions of such arguments? Which ones stood out to you?

5. How do you respond to the idea that evangelism is more of a process? Is this a new concept to you? Is it helpful to think in terms of process rather than event? If so, in what ways?

6. Why are relationships and trust building so crucial to evangelism and apologetics?

7. The chapter discusses idolatry (putting our trust in nonultimate things rather than in God). Do you find this a helpful way to think about connecting people with the gospel? Why or why not?

8. How does seeing Jesus as the climax of history and our highest religious and philosophical ideals help you in thinking of connecting people in your Athens to the gospel?

NOTES

2 WAS PAUL'S SPEECH AT ATHENS A MISTAKE?

[1]Most modern translations use the name in the Greek text of Acts 17:19, Areopagus, while some early translations, such as William Tyndale's New Testament of 1534, have *Marsestrete*. The much more recent *Bible in Basic English* has "Mars Hill."

[2]F. F. Bruce, *Paul: Apostle of the Heart Set Free* (Grand Rapids: Eerdmans, 1977), p. 248.

[3]Ibid., p. 249.

[4]Ibid., p. 245.

[5]Ibid., p. 246.

[6]William Ramsay, *St. Paul the Traveller and the Roman Citizen* (London: Hodder & Stoughton, 1892), p. 252.

[7]Ralph P. Martin, *Acts* (Grand Rapids: Eerdmans, 1967), p. 60.

[8]David K. Clark, "Is Presuppositional Apologetics Rational?" *Bulletin of the Evangelical Philosophical Society* 16 (1993): 12.

[9]N. T. Wright, *Paul in Fresh Perspective* (Minneapolis: Fortress, 2005), p. 105. A couple of helpful essays on Paul's sermon at Athens are J. Daryl Charles's "Paul Before the Areopagus: Reflections on the Apostle's Encounter with Cultured Paganism," *Philosophia Christi* 7, no. 1 (2005): 125-40; and his "Engaging the (Neo) Pagan Mind: Paul's Encounter with Athenian Culture as a Model of Cultural Apologetics," *Trinity Journal* 16 (1995): 47-62.

[10]Bruce Winter makes this point in *After Paul Left Corinth: The Influence of Secular Ethics and Social Change* (Grand Rapids: Eerdmans, 2001), p. 57.

[11]See Anthony Thiselton, "Realized Eschatology at Corinth," *New Testament Studies* 24 (July 1978): 510-26.

[12]We could throw in Paul's citing the Cretan thinker Epimenides in Titus 1:12.

[13]However, the gospel is implied in Paul's speech at Lystra (as at Athens): "In the generations gone by He permitted all the nations to go their own ways" (Acts 14:16 NASB). Compare this with Acts 17:30, where Jesus is specifically mentioned: "Therefore having overlooked the times of ignorance . . ." (NASB).

[14]G. Walter Hansen, "The Preaching and Defence of Paul," in *Witness to the Gospel:*

The Theology of Acts, ed. I. H. Marshall and David Peterson (Grand Rapids: Eerdmans, 1998), pp. 298, 313.

[15]Wright, *Paul,* pp. 3-6.

[16]Ibid., p. 6.

[17]Ben Witherington III, *Paul's Narrative Thought World* (Louisville, KY: Westminster John Knox, 1994), p. 216.

[18]Ibid.

3 Paul's Athens

[1]James D. G. Dunn, *Beginning from Jerusalem,* vol. 2, *Christianity in the Making* (Grand Rapids: Eerdmans, 2009), p. 683.

[2]While there is no firm evidence for an altar to an unknown god in the singular, it is evident from classical texts that authors went back and forth between *god* and *gods* with no explanation; so it is quite plausible that Paul saw an inscription to an unknown god.

[3]See Jaroslav Pelikan, *The Emergence of the Catholic Tradition* (Chicago: University of Chicago Press, 1971), pp. 51-54. The Scriptures emphasize how the body will be raised immortal and incorruptible (1 Cor 15). They also emphasize how God's un-changing nature has more to do with his faithfulness and reliability of character than with his being unmoved by, say, human suffering or evil.

[4]It is noteworthy that there is not any verse in the Bible that says Christians go to heaven when they die. The Bible does teach, however, that believers will one day be given imperishable resurrection bodies in the final state (see 1 Cor 15; Phil 3:21; 1 Thess 4:13-17).

[5]In the second century A.D., this was a key issue for the early Christians. Irenaeus in *Against Heresies* focused on this specific form of false teaching.

[6]Benjamin Wiker makes the connection between ancient and modern-day hedonism. He argues that Epicurus has offered something of a philosophical justification for the hedonistic strain in naturalistic Darwinism today. See his *Moral Darwinism: How We Became Hedonists* (Downers Grove, IL: InterVarsity Press, 2002).

[7]C. Forbes, "Epictetus," in *Dictionary of New Testament Background,* ed. Craig A. Evans and Stanley E. Porter (Downers Grove, IL: InterVarsity Press, 2000), p. 324.

4 Our Athens

[1]The word *Christos* is not a name. It means "anointed one." Anyone familiar with the Scriptures would have understood *Christos* to be equivalent to a Hebrew word that means "anointed one," which is normally rendered in English as the well-known title *Messiah.*

[2]For a discussion on this, see Thomas Sowell, *Intellectuals and Society* (New York: Basic Books, 2012).

[3]Neil Postman, *Amusing Ourselves to Death: Public Discourse in the Age of Show*

Business (New York: Penguin Books, 1985).

[4]Mark Noll, *The Scandal of the Evangelical Mind* (Grand Rapids: Eerdmans, 1995).

[5]Jerome Murphy-O'Connor, *Paul: A Critical Life* (Oxford: Oxford University Press, 1996), p. 108.

[6]Christian philosopher Marilyn McCord Adams takes an unfair jab at Paul: "The Paul of Acts does not pursue his mission to the Athenians, for the simple reason that he was not a philosopher" ("Philosophy and the Bible: The Areopagus Speech," *Faith and Philosophy* 9 [1992]: 146). This, of course, is an argument from silence. Athens was an unplanned, transitional stop, as Paul had been escorted there after trouble in Berea; he was hoping Silas and Timothy would rejoin him there. Furthermore, Paul may not have wanted to stay around to see if the council at Athens would vote in favor of this deity Jesus, whom Paul was presenting. Finally, as we show, Luke portrays Paul as a Christian Socrates.

[7]Taken from G. W. Hansen, "The Preaching and Defence of Paul," in *Witness to the Gospel: The Theology of Acts,* ed. I. Howard Marshall and David Peterson (Grand Rapids: Eerdmans, 1998), p. 310.

[8]Ibid.

[9]Holly Ordway, *Not God's Type: A Rational Academic Finds a Radical Faith* (Chicago: Moody Press, 2010), p. 16.

[10]On this point, see Paul Copan, "The Naturalists Are Declaring the Glory of God: Discovering Natural Theology in the Unlikeliest Places," pp. 50-70 in *Philosophy and the Christian Worldview: Analysis, Assessment and Development,* ed. David Werther and Mark D. Linville (New York: Continuum, 2012).

[11]See Copan, "Naturalists Are Declaring the Glory of God"; J. P. Moreland, *The Recalcitrant Imago Dei: Human Persons and the Failure of Naturalism* (London: SCM Press, 2009); and Paul Copan and William Lane Craig, eds., *Contending with Christianity's Critics* (Nashville: B & H Academic, 2009).

[12]This was evident in the writings of Origen, a third-century church father. In his book *On First Principles,* Origen argued that philosophical methods for establishing truth should be applied to resolving disagreements over Christian doctrines.

[13]For more detailed discussion on Augustine's pilgrimage, see Paul Copan, "The Scandal of the North African Catholic Mind," *Journal of the Evangelical Theological Society* 41 (June 1998): 287-95.

[14]Augustine, *Confessions* 11.12.14.

[15]Augustine, *Gen. litt.* 1.19.39.

[16]Augustine, *Confessions* 10.27.38.

[17]Timothy Lenoir, *The Strategy of Life* (Chicago: University of Chicago Press, 1992), p. ix.

[18]See, for example, N. T. Wright, *The Resurrection of the Son of God* (Minneapolis: Fortress, 2003); Gary R. Habermas and Michael R. Licona, *The Case for the Resur-*

rection of Jesus (Grand Rapids: Kregel, 2004); Michael R. Licona, *The Resurrection of Jesus: A New Historiographical Approach* (Downers Grove, IL: IVP Academic, 2010); William Lane Craig, *Assessing the New Testament Evidence for the Historicity of the Resurrection of Jesus* (Lewiston, NY: Mellen, 1989); and Craig Keener, *Miracles* (Grand Rapids: Baker Academic, 2011).

[19]Wright, *Resurrection of the Son of God*, p. 710.

[20]Rodney Stark, *The Victory of Reason* (New York: Random House, 2005), p. xi.

[21]Paul Davies, *Are We Alone?* (New York: Basic Books, 1995), p. 96.

[22]J. Robert Oppenheimer refers to "an idea of progress which has more to do with the human condition," expressed by the Christian understanding of "works"—"the notion that the betterment of man's condition, his civility, had meaning; that we all had a responsibility to it, a duty to it, and to man" ("On Science and Culture," *Encounter* 19 [October 1962]: 5). This was not something present in ancient Chinese, Indian and Greco-Roman civilization.

[23]Jürgen Habermas, *Time of Transitions,* ed. and trans. Ciaran Cronin and Max Pensky (Cambridge: Polity, 2006), pp. 150-51.

[24]Jacques Derrida, "To Forgive: The Unforgivable and Imprescriptable," in *Questioning God*, ed. John D. Caupto et al. (Bloomington: Indiana University Press, 2001), p. 70.

[25]See Mario Beauregard and Denyse O'Leary, *The Spiritual Brain: A Neuroscientist's Case for the Existence of the Soul* (New York: HarperOne, 2008); Mario Beauregard, *Brain Wars: The Scientific Battle over the Existence of the Mind and the Proof That Will Change the Way We Live Our Lives* (New York: HarperOne, 2012); and Jeffrey M. Schwartz and Beverly Beyette, *Brain Lock: Free Yourself from Obsessive-Compulsive Disorder* (New York: Harper Perennial, 2007).

[26]See the *Journal of Near Death Experiences* as well as Michael Sabom, *Light and Death* (Grand Rapids: Zondervan, 1998).

[27]Priscilla K. Coleman, "Abortion and Mental Health: Quantitative Synthesis and Analysis of Research Published 1995–2009," *British Journal of Psychiatry* 199 (2011): 180-86. Also see Nancy Moore Clatworthy, "The Case Against Living Together" (interview), *Seventeen,* November 1977, pp. 132-33, 162-63; and D. P. Orr, M. Beiter and G. Ingersoll, "Premature Sexual Activity as an Indicator of Psychological Risk," *Pediatrics* 87 (February 1991): 141-47.

[28]Alvin Goldman, *Knowledge in a Social World* (Oxford: Oxford University Press, 1999), p. 20.

[29]Ibid., p. 21.

[30]Richard Rorty, *Philosophy and the Mirror of Nature* (Princeton: Princeton University Press, 1979), pp. 175-76.

[31]See J. P. Moreland's *Love Your God with All Your Mind* (Colorado Springs: NavPress, 1997) on the "I think" versus "I feel" distinction.

[32]See Neil Postman, *Amusing Ourselves to Death,* 2nd ed. (New York: Penguin, 2005).

[33]See N. T. Wright, *After You Believe: Why Christian Character Matters* (New York: HarperOne, 2010), pp. 154-59.

[34]This statement was aired on *The Oprah Winfrey Show* (Harpo Productions), Thursday, February 15, 2007.

[35]Dalai Lama, *Kindness, Clarity and Insight* (New York: Snow Lion, 1984), p. 45.

[36]For further discussion on pluralism, see Paul Copan, *"True for You, but Not for Me": Overcoming Objections to Christian Faith* (Minneapolis: Bethany House, 2009).

[37]Barna Group, "Americans Draw Theological Beliefs from Diverse Points of View," October 8, 2002, www.barna.org/barna-update/article/5-barna-update/82 -americans-draw-theological-beliefs-from-diverse-points-of-view; and Barna Group, "Barna Survey Examines Changes in Worldview Among Christians over the Past 13 Years," March 6, 2009, www.barna.org/barna-update/article /21-transformation/252-barna-survey-examines-changes-in-worldview-among -christians-over-the-past-13-years.

[38]The apologist is Ravi Zacharias. See his summary of this conversation in "Words, Bodies, and Spirit" at Slice of Infinity (October 20, 2011), www.rzim.org/a-slice -of-infinity/words-bodies-and-spirit.

[39]Michael W. Goheen and Craig G. Bartholomew, *Living at the Crossroads: An Introduction to Christian Worldview* (Grand Rapids: Baker Academic, 2008), p. 23.

[40]Alfred North Whitehead, *Science and the Modern World* (New York: Mentor, 1952), pp. 49-50.

[41]Stephen Hawking, *A Brief History of Time* (New York: Bantam, 1988), p. 13.

[42]Richard Dawkins, *River out of Eden: A Darwinian View of Life* (New York: Basic Books, 1995), p. 33.

[43]Richard Lewontin, "Billions and Billions of Demons," *New York Review of Books,* January 9, 1997, pp. 28-32.

[44]Ibid., pp. 28, 31.

[45]Alvin Plantinga, *Where the Conflict Really Lies* (New York: Oxford University Press, 2012).

[46]Del Ratzsch, *Philosophy of Science* (Downers Grove, IL: InterVarsity Press, 1986), p. 15.

[47]This quotation is from John Post, *Metaphysics: A Contemporary Introduction* (New York: Paragon House, 1991), p. 85.

[48]Cited in Gerard M. Verschuuren, *What Makes You Tick? A New Paradigm for Neuroscience* (Antioch, CA: Solas, 2012), p. viii.

[49]Stanley Jaki, *The Savior of Science* (Washington: Regnery, 1988).

5 PAUL'S SPEECHES IN ACTS

[1]While we usually call those who write about the past *historians* and restrict the

term *historiography* to the study of how to write history, authors like Thucydides, Seutonius, Josephus and many others begin their works with (usually long) prefaces that describe how they have gone about the task of recounting history. Hence, it is proper to refer to them as historiographers, for they are as concerned about how they write and how they obtained their information as they are with what they write.

[2]For further reading in support of this understanding of what Thucydides sought to do when recounting speeches, see F. F. Bruce, "Paul's Apologetic and the Purpose of Acts," *Bulletin of the John Rylands University Library of Manchester* 69 (1987): 373n2.

[3]The one place that may, in the minds of some, provide evidence of a mistake on Luke's part is in the speech of Gamaliel in Acts 5:34-39. Gamaliel speaks of a Theudas who was a messianic pretender before the time of one Judas. Josephus, using the same names, places a Judas and a Theudas in the opposite order. This is used by many scholars to show that Luke did not have his facts straight. We only have the accounts in Acts and Josephus on this small issue. Since there is not a third source that might help us determine which order is correct historically, and since Josephus himself is known to make mistakes and exaggerations, it is not proper to assume that Josephus is right and Luke is wrong. We simply cannot demonstrate either way what the correct order ought to be; so this small detail should not be used to assess the historical reliability of Acts. Or, perhaps it is the case that Luke correctly reported Gamaliel's words, even if Gamaliel made a mistake.

[4]See especially the extensive treatment of several historical issues in Craig S. Keener, *Acts: An Exegetical Commentary*, vol. 1, *Introduction and 1:1–2:47* (Grand Rapids: Baker Academic, 2012), pp. 3-382; Colin J. Hemer, *The Book of Acts in the Setting of Hellenistic History*, ed. Conrad H. Gempf (Tübingen: Mohr, 1989); and I. Howard Marshall, *Luke: Historian and Theologian*, rev. ed. (Downers Grove, IL: InterVarsity Press, 1998).

[5]The Sanhedrin was the supreme governing body within Judaism and was responsible for many political and theological matters under the authority of Roman proconsuls.

[6]In a literary context, a quotation may be thought of as a direct quote of a biblical text, usually with a citation formula, such as, "it is written." An allusion is close to a direct quotation but lacks some words or substitutes other words so that it is clear what verse it is based upon. An echo represents enough words to evoke one or more verses from Scripture, but it is not always clear which verse the speaker/writer may have had in mind. Biblical themes depend not so much upon wording but upon larger concepts that exist in a passage. For more on the concept of echo, see Richard B. Hays, *Echoes of Scripture in the Letters of Paul* (New Haven, CT: Yale University Press, 1989); and based upon Hays's understanding of echoes, Kenneth

D. Litwak, *Echoes of Scripture in Luke-Acts: Telling the Story of God's People Inter-textually* (London: T & T Clark, 2005); and especially Kenneth D. Litwak, "Israel's Prophets Meet Athens' Philosophers: Scriptural Echoes in Acts 17,22-31," *Biblica* 85 (2004): 199-216.

[7]A God-fearer was someone who was attracted to the teachings and ethics of Judaism but was not willing to become a full proselyte. For men, becoming a proselyte (a convert) to Judaism required getting circumcised.

[8]Kathy Maxwell, *Hearing Between the Lines: The Audience as Fellow-Worker in Luke-Acts and Its Literary Milieu* (London: T & T Clark, 2010), p. 35. Maxwell provides a detailed description of what Greco-Roman writers on the subject of rhetoric said in relation to the audience (*Hearing Between the Lines,* pp. 27-78).

[9]For further discussion on this, see chapter one.

[10]For a more detailed treatment of this issue, see Conrad Gempf, "Before Paul Arrived in Corinth: The Mission Strategies in 1 Corinthians 2:2 and Acts 17," in *The New Testament in Its First Century Setting: Essays on Context and Background in Honour of B. W. Winter on His 65th Birthday,* ed. P. J. Williams et al. (Grand Rapids: Eerdmans, 2004), pp. 126-42.

[11]An orator's speech would be evaluated by an audience in part on whether the speech followed standard rhetorical convention as defined by authors such as Cicero, Aristotle and Quintilian. In terms of rhetoric, creativity was not valued highly.

[12]See David E. Aune, *The New Testament in Its Literary Environment* (Philadelphia: Westminster, 1989), pp. 60-65, 95-96; and Todd Penner, *In Praise of Christian Origins: Stephen and the Hellenists in Lukan Apologetic Historiography* (London: T & T Clark, 2004), pp. 147-79.

[13]George A. Kennedy, *New Testament Interpretation Through Rhetorical Criticism* (Chapel Hill: University of North Carolina Press, 1984), p. 129.

[14]It might be that the "disciples" of Acts 14:20 are converts who accepted Paul's message in Lystra, but the word could as easily refer to the other people who traveled with Paul on his journey.

6 PAUL'S AUDIENCE

[1]See Paul Copan, "Want the Bad News First?" *Patheos,* March 16, 2010, www.patheos.com/Resources/Additional-Resources/Want-the-Bad-News-First?print=1.

[2]On relationships, see Win Arn and Charles Arn, *The Master's Plan for Making Disciples: Every Christian an Effective Witness Through an Enabling Church,* 2nd ed. (Grand Rapids: Baker Books, 1998); on felt needs, see David Bennett's research at the Bridge Builders website: www.bridge-builders.net/current/howadults.php.

[3]See Nabeel Jabbour, *The Crescent Through the Eyes of the Cross* (Colorado Springs: NavPress, 2008).

[4]See David Kinnaman and Gabe Lyons, *Unchristian: What a New Generation Really*

Thinks About Christianity—and Why It Matters (Grand Rapids: Baker Books, 2007); and David Kinnaman with Aly Hawkins, *You Lost Me: Why Young Christians Are Leaving the Church—and Rethinking Faith* (Grand Rapids: Baker Books, 2011).

[5]See Patrick Gray for further discussion of this important point in "Implied Audiences in the Areopagus Narrative," *Tyndale Bulletin* 55 (2004): 210.

[6]Bertil E. Gärtner, *The Areopagus Speech and Natural Revelation*, trans. Carolyn Hannay King (Uppsala: Gleerup, 1955), p. 106.

[7]*Deum te igitur scito esse* (know then that you are a god), Cicero, *Rep.* 6.26.

[8]While major cities such as Athens and Thessalonica placed heavy emphasis on the imperial cult and enjoyed some benefits of Roman control, other places did not fare so well. The first-century A.D. Roman historian Tacitus wrote of the liberty of the native peoples of Germanica and ancient England, in contrast to the harsh rule of the Roman Empire over these areas. According to Tacitus, Calgacus, a chieftain in northern Scotland, said of the Pax Romana, "To ravage, to slaughter, to usurp under false titles, they call empire; and where they make a desert, they call it peace" (*Agricola* 29-32).

[9]Bruce W. Winter, "Introducing the Athenians to God: Paul's Failed Apologetic in Acts 17," *Themelios* 31, no. 1 (2005): 44.

[10]It is not, however, essential for understanding Paul's speech to know whether he had to answer for his attempted role as the proclaimer of foreign deities. The approach and content of the speech remain the same, but part of Paul's rhetorical goal may have been different. See Bruce W. Winter, "In Public and in Private: Early Christians and Religious Pluralism," in *One God, One Lord: Christianity in a World of Religious Pluralism*, ed. Andrew D. Clarke and Bruce W. Winter (Grand Rapids: Baker Books, 1992), p. 127, especially nn. 5 and 6, where Winter argues for the possibility that Paul was invited to present his credentials as an orator to the Areopagus. It was customary for a traveling orator, when he arrived in a city, to present his credentials to the local city council or some group of invited citizens. The invitation to speak before the city council was extended regularly to any public orator when he arrived in a city in the eastern part of the Roman Empire.

[11]For a thorough, detailed description of views of the afterlife among non-Jews in Paul's day, see the very valuable study by N. T. Wright, *The Resurrection of the Son of God* (Minneapolis: Fortress, 2003), pp. 38-84. Wright's work is not to be missed by anyone who wants to understand the meaning of *resurrection* in the Greco-Roman world and alternative views of the afterlife.

[12]Aeschylus, *Eum.* 647-48, quoted from Winter, "Introducing the Athenians to God," p. 47.

[13]Paul uses is the word *adelphoi*, "brothers," but in many contexts, such as 1 Corinthians 1, it almost certainly bears the sense of "brothers and sisters," a usage well known from Greek authors outside of the New Testament. This word can be used

for a brother, brother and sister in the plural form, member, associate, or compatriot. Paul did not use the word *adelphoi* in order to point to only one gender but followed cultural practice in using the word for all the believers in Corinth regardless of gender.

7 PAUL'S GOSPEL FOR THE EDUCATED

[1]N. T. Wright, "Jesus and the Identity of God," *Ex Auditu* 14 (1998): 44.

[2]The word *emptiness* is a translation of the Hebrew word *hebel,* which is used repeatedly in the book of Ecclesiastes. There it states that learning, luxury, lust and labor are all emptiness or meaninglessness. Ultimately what matters is fearing God and keeping his commandments (Eccles 12:13).

[3]On the jealousy of God, see Paul Copan, *Is God a Moral Monster? Understanding the Old Testament God* (Grand Rapids: Baker, 2011), chap. 4.

[4]See also Deuteronomy 4:25 and 6:15.

[5]See, for example, 1 Kings 14:21.

[6]Miroslav Volf, *Free of Charge: Giving and Forgiving in a Culture Stripped of Grace* (Grand Rapids: Zondervan, 2006), pp. 138-39.

[7]On this point, see C. Stephen Evans, *Natural Signs and Knowledge of God: A New Look at Theistic Arguments* (New York: Oxford University Press, 2012).

[8]From Blaise Pascal's classic *Pensées,* #430.

[9]*Christ* is not Jesus' last name. It is the Greek word for "anointed one" and is roughly equivalent to *Messiah,* the Hebrew word for "anointed one." Since Paul specifically refers to Jesus with this title, *Christos* is best rendered by *Messiah.*

[10]"This world-order [*kosmos*], the same of all, no god nor man did create, but it ever was and is and will be: everliving fire, kindling in measures and being quenched in measures." This is from B30, one of the many fragments of his work. Daniel W. Graham, "Heraclitus," *The Stanford Encyclopedia of Philosophy* (Summer 2011 ed.), http://plato.stanford.edu/archives/sum2011/entries/heraclitus.

8 THE ART OF PERSUASION

[1]Donald Miller, *Blue Like Jazz* (Nashville: Thomas Nelson, 2003), p. 115.

[2]Jews were known for their odd habit of taking the seventh day of each week as a rest day; there was no concept in Greek culture of weekends being time off from work. Jews were also noteworthy for refusing to eat pork (a very popular meat among Gentiles). Rather than obtaining meat from the marketplace that might violate Mosaic instructions for preparation—such as not having the blood drained, being killed by strangling or being offered first to an idol—the Jews got special permission from the Romans to slaughter their own clean animals in ways that observed the law of Moses. To many, Jews also appeared to be atheists, just as Christians were later seen, because they worshiped only one god and rejected the traditional Greek pantheon. Since they would not worship the emperor either, they

often appeared to be bad citizens who cared nothing for the welfare of their city or town. In some instances, there was great animosity toward Jews for their odd behavior and beliefs, but many Gentiles admired Jewish morals.

[3]Some helpful commentaries on Acts, going from less detailed to more detailed, include I. Howard Marshall, *Acts: An Introduction and Commentary,* Tyndale New Testament Commentary 5 (Downers Grove, IL: IVP Academic, 2008); David G. Peterson, *The Acts of the Apostles,* Pillar New Testament Commentary (Grand Rapids: Eerdmans, 2009); and Ben Witherington III, *The Acts of the Apostles: A Socio-Rhetorical Commentary* (Grand Rapids: Eerdmans, 1998).

[4]For a thorough treatment of rhetoric and its elements, see, for example, the four-volume work by Quintilian, *The Instituto Oratoria of Quintilian, with an English Translation,* trans. H. E. Butler (Cambridge, MA: Harvard University Press, 1953).

[5]C. Kavin Rowe, *World Upside Down: Reading Acts in the Greco-Roman Age* (Oxford: Oxford University Press, 2009), p. 28.

[6]The Apocrypha represent a collection of books that were never accepted by Jews as Scripture but were accepted by many Christians as profitable, and therefore Christians, rather than Jews, put these books into their Bibles. The earliest known complete Bibles, written in Greek, contain these books. The Apocrypha are included in the Bibles of many Christian traditions, such as Roman Catholic Bibles. Most Protestant Bibles do not contain these books. The full story, however, is much more complex. For further information, see David A. deSilva, *Introducing the Apocrypha: Message, Context, and Significance* (Grand Rapids: Baker Academic, 2002).

[7]For a detailed treatment of the use of scriptural echoes in Paul's speech, see Kenneth D. Litwak, "Israel's Prophets Meet Athens' Philosophers: Scriptural Echoes in Acts 17,22-31," *Biblica* 85 (2004): 199-216.

[8]Here Paul expresses the idea that all people are God's offspring, that he gives them the gift of existence. This does not mean, as is clear in Acts 17:30-31, that being God's offspring in this sense is sufficient. Instead, we must repent and turn to God in order to be brought into his family by regeneration. Cf. Romans 8:12-17, where Paul talks about believers being adopted into God's family, which is not something automatically given to all. Paul uses the language of sonship in Romans 8 because in Paul's world only boys were adopted, not because God thinks less of women.

[9]The Hellenistic historiographer Polybius says that it is the "superstition" (*deisidaimonia*) of the Romans that is at once a cause for the reproach aimed at the Romans among other peoples and that "which maintains cohesions of the Roman state" (*Historia,* 6.56 LCL). The same word is used in Acts 25:19 in a positive way.

[10]See the references to Greco-Roman authors in Colin J. Hemer, *The Book of Acts in the Setting of Hellenistic Historiography,* ed. Conrad H. Gempf (Winona Lake, IN: Eisenbrauns, 1990), p. 117.

[11]F. F. Bruce, *The Acts of the Apostles: The Greek Text with Introduction and Commentary* (Grand Rapids: Eerdmans, 1951), p. 336.

[12]See also Genesis 14:19, 22 and Exodus 20:11, which asserts that "in six days the LORD made heaven and earth and the seas and everything in them." Psalm 145:6 states that God made the heavens, the earth, the seas and everything in them.

[13]John B. Polhill, *Acts*, New American Commentary 26 (Nashville: B & H Academic, 1992), p. 374.

[14]Apuleius, *Metamorphoses*, XI.5.

[15]Cf. Isaiah 58:2, Jeremiah 50:4; Ezekiel 20:40 and 34:11; Daniel 9:3; Hosea 3:5; and Amos 5:14.

[16]Cf. 2 Chronicles 14:4; 15:12-13; 19:3; 26:5; 30:19 and 34:3.

[17]Cf. Psalm 62:1; 68:7, 33; and 69:5.

[18]This is similar to a common inscription on Hellenistic tombs.

[19]English Bible translations typically render the opening words of Acts 17:28 as "for in him we live." The Greek text could mean "in the sphere of influence," which would mean that God influences human life, activity and existence. It can however, have an instrumental force. In this case, "him" would be the means by which humans live, act and exist. While the grammar would normally require an impersonal means, it appears that Paul is making a compressed statement, which would be expanded to "for by/in the power of [God] we live and act and exist." The original Greek poet might well have meant "in God" but had the Stoic pantheistic meaning of "god" as the entire environment of which humans are a part. Paul would never mean that. Therefore, it seems best to see that he used the words of a Greek poet but filled them with Jewish-Christian meaning. God is transcendent above all and separate from all things. He is near to humans but not in the pantheistic way that the Stoics would have seen this.

[20]See Clement of Alexandria, *Stromata* 1.14, 19.

[21]We know of the text of the *Phaenomena* because it was preserved by a second-century B.C. Hellenistic Jewish writer, Aristobulus, whose writings we know because they were partially preserved by the Christian writer Eusebius.

[22]Paul is not talking about humans as God's children in the same sense as the language of sonship in Romans 8. Paul is only seeking to use Stoic statements as rhetorical proofs for his belief that God made humans.

9 ACTING ON THE TRUTH

[1]Still less so to follow the maxim *Credo quia absurdum* ("I believe because it is absurd").

[2]*Theion* is the neuter form of an adjective, which means "divine," though it can also be used as a noun for "divine nature." This word is used only three times in any form in the New Testament, here in Acts 17:29 and in 2 Peter 1:3-4 to refer to God's power and nature. The word is also used in the Old Testament five times (not

counting 4 Maccabees, a very Hellenistic work that was never part of the Jewish Scripture). It is clear that *theion* is not the common biblical word for God; so Paul has very deliberately chosen it to speak with Greek philosophical language to his audience, who would have known little to nothing of the Scriptures of Israel. When referring to God, Paul regularly uses *theos*. While there is probably significance in the choice of gender of both of these words, no argument should be made based upon the grammatical gender alone.

[3]The only other place in the New Testament that uses this word is 2 Peter 1:3, where it fills its normal role as an adjective, "As everything has been given to us by his divine power for the purpose of life and godliness."

[4]Compare the similar vocabulary and polemic in Isaiah 44:9-20 and 46:5-6.

[5]Cf. for example Ezekiel 16:38 and 24:14 and Habakkuk 1:2-17.

10 Going to Our Own Mars Hill

[1]For a critique of various forms of relativism, see Paul Copan, *"True for You, but Not for Me": Overcoming Objections to Christian Faith* (Minneapolis: Bethany House, 2009).

[2]Clifford Williams, *Existential Reasons for Belief in God* (Downers Grove, IL: Inter-Varsity Press, 2011).

[3]Cited in ibid., p. 50.

[4]C. S. Lewis, "The Weight of Glory," in *The Weight of Glory and Other Addresses* (New York: Macmillan, 1965), pp. 6-7.

[5]Ibid., p. 7; emphasis in original.

[6]Augustine, *Confessions* 1.1.

[7]Greg Ganssle, "Making the Gospel Connection," in *Come Let Us Reason: New Essays in Christian Apologetics,* ed. Paul Copan and William Lane Craig (Nashville: B & H Academic, 2012), pp. 13-14.

[8]J. Gresham Machen, "Christianity and Culture," *Princeton Theological Review* 11 (1913): 7.

[9]Ibid.

[10]Greg Koukl uses the image of a pebble in the shoe in his book *Tactics* (Grand Rapids: Zondervan, 2008).

[11]Paul Copan has been involved in leading a Socrates Café in West Palm Beach, Florida. See www.meetup.com/Socrates-Cafe-in-West-Palm-Beach-FL.

[12]The philosopher William Lane Craig has initiated Reasonable Faith chapters that gather monthly to discuss apologetical/philosophical topics. Craig has written an apologetics book, *Reasonable Faith: Christian Truth and Apologetics,* 3rd ed. (Wheaton, IL: Crossway, 2008), and the more accessible *On Guard: Defending Your Faith with Reason and Precision* (Colorado Springs: David C. Cook, 2010). See Craig's website, www.reasonablefaith.org, for many valuable resources. Also, the Christian author and speaker Eric Metaxas has hosted Socrates in the City in New

York with great success. See www.socratesinthecity.com.

[13]These steps are taken from Don Everts and Doug Schaupp, *I Once Was Lost: What Postmodern Skeptics Taught Us About Their Path to Jesus* (Downers Grove, IL: InterVarsity Press, 2008).

[14]For a response to *Zeitgeist* and the dying-and-rising god idea, see the essays by Mark W. Foreman, "Challenging the Zeitgeist Move: Parallelomania on Steroids," pp. 169-187, and Mary Jo Sharp, "Does the Story of Jesus Mimic Pagan Mystery Stories?," pp. 151-68 in *Come Let Us Reason*, ed. Paul Copan and William Lane Craig (Nashville: B & H Academic, 2012); and Stanley E. Porter and Stephen J. Bedard, *Unmasking the Pagan Christ: An Evangelical Response to the Cosmic Christ Idea* (Bowmanville, ON: Clements Publishing Group, 2006). N. T. Wright said that attempts to draw parallels between Christianity and these mystery religions "have failed, as virtually all Pauline scholars now recognize" and that to do so "is an attempt to turn the clock back in a way now forbidden by the most massive and learned studies on the subject" (*What Saint Paul Really Said* [Grand Rapids: Eerdmans, 1997], pp. 172-73).

[15]Michael Grant, *Jesus: An Historian's Review of the Gospels* (New York: Scribner's, 1992), p. 199. Further, we don't need to resort to paganism at all. To use the same terms, like *mystery* or *salvation*, is different from saying they're the same concepts. We could add that the Old Testament/Jewish background to the Gospels gives a sufficient context for explaining such a high Christology: Richard Bauckham, *Jesus and the God of Israel: God Crucified and Other Studies on the New Testament's Christology of Divine Identity* (Grand Rapids: Eerdmans, 2008). Furthermore, those pagan parallels really only emerge in the second to fourth centuries A.D., and scholars have a hunch that the spread of Christianity in the Mediterranean world gave rise to these alleged parallels rather than the reverse. If anything, the Christian faith influenced these pagan dying-and-rising-god myths.

[16]David Pao, *Acts and the Isaianic New Exodus* (Grand Rapids: Baker Academic, 2002), pp. 193-97.

[17]Thomas Nagel, *The Last Word* (New York: Oxford University Press, 1997), p. 130.

[18]Ibid., p. 131.

[19]Aldous Huxley, *Ends and Means* (London: Chatto & Windus, 1969), pp. 270, 273.

[20]Tim Keller, "The Gospel in All Its Forms," *Leadership Journal* 29, no. 2 (2008): 15, www.christianitytoday.com/le/2008/spring/9.74a.html.

[21]See Craig M. Gay, *The Way of the (Modern) World: Or, Why It's Tempting to Live as If God Doesn't Exist* (Grand Rapids: Eerdmans, 1998).

[22]See Colin Gunton, *Act and Being* (Grand Rapids: Eerdmans, 2003), p. 282.

[23]C. S. Lewis, "Myth Became Fact," in *C. S. Lewis Essay Collection: Faith, Christianity and the Church*, ed. Lesley Walmsley (London: HarperCollins, 2002), pp. 138-42.

[24]William L. Lane, *Hebrews 1–8*, Word Biblical Commentary 47A (Dallas: Word, 1991), pp. 56-57.

[25]Some of the points in the following paragraphs are taken from Jaroslav Pelikan, *Jesus Through the Centuries* (New York: Harper & Row, 1987), chap. 3.

[26]Ibid., p. 31.

[27]Ibid., p. 34.

[28]J. R. R. Tolkien, "On Fairy Stories." Available at various places on the Internet; for example, http://brainstorm-services.com/wcu-2004/fairystories-tolkien.pdf.

BIBLIOGRAPHY

Adams, Marilyn McCord. "Philosophy and the Bible: The Areopagus Speech." *Faith and Philosophy* 9 (1992): 135-50.

Arn, Win, and Charles Arn. *The Master's Plan for Making Disciples: Every Christian an Effective Witness Through an Enabling Church.* 2nd ed. Grand Rapids: Baker Books, 1998.

Aune, David E. *The New Testament in Its Literary Environment.* Philadelphia: Westminster, 1989.

Barna Group. "Americans Draw Theological Beliefs from Diverse Points of View." October 8, 2002. www.barna.org/barna-update/article/5-barna-update/82 -americans-draw-theological-beliefs-from-diverse-points-of-view.

———. "Barna Survey Examines Changes in Worldview Among Christians over the Past 13 Years." March 6, 2009. www.barna.org/barna-update/article/21-transformation /252-barna-survey-examines-changes-in-worldview-among-christians-over-the -past-13-years.

Bauckham, Richard. *Jesus and the God of Israel: God Crucified and Other Studies on the New Testament's Christology of Divine Identity.* Grand Rapids: Eerdmans, 2008.

Bauer, W., F. W. Danker, W. F. Arndt and F. W. Gingrich. *A Greek-English Lexicon of the New Testament and Other Early Christian Literature.* 3rd ed. Chicago: University of Chicago Press, 2001.

Beauregard, Mario. *Brain Wars: The Scientific Battle over the Existence of the Mind and the Proof That Will Change the Way We Live Our Lives.* New York: HarperOne, 2012.

Beauregard, Mario, and Denyse O'Leary. *The Spiritual Brain: A Neuroscientist's Case for the Existence of the Soul.* New York: HarperOne, 2008.

Bruce, F. F. *The Acts of the Apostles: The Greek Test with Introduction and Commentary.* Grand Rapids: Eerdmans, 1951.

———. *Paul: Apostle of the Heart Set Free.* Grand Rapids: Eerdmans, 1977.

———. "Paul's Apologetic and the Purpose of Acts." *Bulletin of the John Rylands University Library of Manchester* 69 (1987): 379-93.

Charles, J. Daryl. "Engaging the (Neo)Pagan Mind: Paul's Encounter with Athenian Culture as a Model of Cultural Apologetics." *Trinity Journal* 16 (1995): 47-62.

———. "Paul Before the Areopagus: Reflections on the Apostle's Encounter with Cultured Paganism." *Philosophia Christi* 7, no. 1 (2005): 125-40.

Clark, David K. "Is Presuppositional Apologetics Rational?" *Bulletin of the Evangelical Philosophical Society* 16 (1993).

Clatworthy, Nancy Moore. "The Case Against Living Together" (interview). *Seventeen*, November 1977, pp. 132-33, 162-63.

Coleman, Priscilla K. "Abortion and Mental Health: Quantitative Synthesis and Analysis of Research Published 1995–2009." *British Journal of Psychiatry* 199 (2011): 180-86.

Copan, Paul. *Is God a Moral Monster? Understanding the Old Testament God.* Grand Rapids: Baker, 2011.

———. "The Naturalists Are Declaring the Glory of God: Discovering Natural Theology in the Unlikeliest Places." In *Philosophy and the Christian Worldview: Analysis, Assessment and Development,* edited by David Werther and Mark D. Linville, pp. 50-70. New York: Continuum, 2012.

———. "The Scandal of the North African Catholic Mind." *Journal of the Evangelical Theological Society* 41 (June 1998): 287-95.

———. *"True for You, but Not for Me": Overcoming Objections to Christian Faith.* Minneapolis: Bethany House, 2009.

———. "Want the Bad News First?" *Patheos,* March 16, 2010. www.patheos.com /Resources/Additional-Resources/Want-the-Bad-News-First?print=1.

Copan, Paul, and William Lane Craig, eds. *Contending with Christianity's Critics.* Nashville: B & H Academic, 2009.

Craig, William Lane. *Assessing the New Testament Evidence for the Historicity of the Resurrection of Jesus.* Lewiston, NY: Mellen, 1989.

———. *On Guard: Defending Your Faith with Reason and Precision.* Colorado Springs: David C. Cook, 2010.

———. *Reasonable Faith: Christian Truth and Apologetics.* 3rd ed. Wheaton, IL: Crossway, 2008.

Dalai Lama. *Kindness, Clarity and Insight.* New York: Snow Lion, 1984.

Davies, Paul. *Are We Alone?* New York: Basic Books, 1995.

Dawkins, Richard. *River out of Eden: A Darwinian View of Life.* New York: Basic Books, 1995.

deSilva, David A. *Introducing the Apocrypha: Message, Context, and Significance.* Grand Rapids: Baker Academic, 2002.

Dunn, James D. G. *Beginning from Jerusalem.* Vol. 2, *Christianity in the Making.* Grand Rapids: Eerdmans, 2009.

Evans, C. Stephen. *Natural Signs and Knowledge of God: A New Look at Theistic Arguments.* New York: Oxford University Press, 2012.

Everts, Don, and Doug Schaupp. *I Once Was Lost: What Postmodern Skeptics Taught Us About Their Path to Jesus.* Downers Grove, IL: InterVarsity Press, 2008.

Forbes, C. "Epictetus." In *Dictionary of New Testament Background,* edited by Craig A. Evans and Stanley E. Porter, p. 324. Downers Grove, IL: InterVarsity Press, 2000.

Foreman, Mark W. "Challenging the Zeitgeist Move: Parallelomania on Steroids." In *Come Let Us Reason,* edited by Paul Copan and William Lane Craig, pp. 169-87. Nashville: B & H Academic, 2012.

Ganssle, Greg. "Making the Gospel Connection: An Essay Concerning Applied Apologetics." In *Come Let Us Reason: New Essays in Christian Apologetics,* edited by Paul Copan and William Lane Craig, pp. 3-16. Nashville: B & H Academic, 2012.

Gärtner, Bertil. *The Areopagus Speech and Natural Revelation.* Translated by Carolyn H. King. Uppsala: Gleerup, 1955.

Gay, Craig M. *The Way of the (Modern) World: Or, Why It's Tempting to Live as If God Doesn't Exist.* Grand Rapids: Eerdmans, 1998.

Gempf, Conrad. "Before Paul Arrived in Corinth: The Mission Strategies in 1 Corinthians 2:2 and Acts 17." In *The New Testament in Its First Century Setting: Essays on Context and Background in Honour of B. W. Winter on His 65th Birthday,* edited by P. J. Williams et al., pp. 126-42. Grand Rapids: Eerdmans, 2004.

Goheen, Michael W., and Craig G. Bartholomew. *Living at the Crossroads: An Introduction to Christian Worldview.* Grand Rapids: Baker Academic, 2008.

Goldman, Alvin. *Knowledge in a Social World.* Oxford: Oxford University Press, 1999.

Grant, Michael. *Jesus: An Historian's Review of the Gospels.* New York: Scribner's, 1992.

Gray, Patrick. "Implied Audiences in the Areopagus Narrative." *Tyndale Bulletin* 55 (2004): 205-18.

Gunton, Colin. *Act and Being.* Grand Rapids: Eerdmans, 2003.

Habermas, Gary R., and Michael R. Licona. *The Case for the Resurrection of Jesus.* Grand Rapids: Kregel, 2004.

Habermas, Jürgen. *Time of Transitions.* Edited and translated by Ciaran Cronin and Max Pensky. Cambridge: Polity, 2006.

Hansen, G. Walter. "The Preaching and Defence of Paul." In *Witness to the Gospel: The Theology of Acts,* edited by I. H. Marshall and David Peterson, pp. 295-324. Grand Rapids: Eerdmans, 1998.

Hawking, Stephen. *A Brief History of Time.* New York: Bantam, 1988.

Hays, Richard B. *Echoes of Scripture in the Letters of Paul.* New Haven, CT: Yale University Press, 1989.

Hemer, Colin J. *The Book of Acts in the Setting of Hellenistic History.* Edited by Conrad H. Gempf. Tübingen: Mohr, 1989. Winona Lake, IN: Eisenbrauns, 1990.

Huxley, Aldous. *Ends and Means.* London: Chatto & Windus, 1969.

Jabbour, Nabeel. *The Crescent Through the Eyes of the Cross.* Colorado Springs: NavPress, 2008.

Jaki, Stanley. *The Savior of Science.* Washington: Regnery, 1988.

Keener, Craig S. *Acts: An Exegetical Commentary.* Vol. 1, *Introduction and 1:1-2:47.* Grand Rapids: Baker Academic, 2012.

Keener, Craig. *Miracles.* Grand Rapids: Baker Academic, 2011.

Keller, Tim. "The Gospel in All Its Forms." *Leadership Journal* 29, no. 2 (2008): 15. www.christianitytoday.com/le/2008/spring/9.74a.html.

Kennedy, George A. *New Testament Interpretation Through Rhetorical Criticism.* Chapel Hill: University of North Carolina Press, 1984.

Kinnaman, David, and Gabe Lyons. *Unchristian: What a New Generation Really Thinks About Christianity—and Why It Matters.* Grand Rapids: Baker Books, 2007.

Kinnaman, David, with Aly Hawkins. *You Lost Me: Why Young Christians Are Leaving the Church—and Rethinking Faith.* Grand Rapids: Baker Books, 2011.

Koukl, Greg. *Tactics.* Grand Rapids: Zondervan, 2008.

Lane, William L. *Hebrews 1-8.* Word Biblical Commentary 47A. Dallas: Word, 1991.

Lenoir, Timothy. *The Strategy of Life.* Chicago: University of Chicago Press, 1992.

Lewis, C. S. "The Weight of Glory." In *The Weight of Glory and Other Addresses.* New York: Macmillan, 1965.

Lewontin, Richard. "Billions and Billions of Demons." *New York Review of Books,* January 9, 1997, pp. 28-32.

Licona, Michael R. *The Resurrection of Jesus: A New Historiographical Approach.* Downers Grove, IL: IVP Academic, 2010.

Litwak, Kenneth D. *Echoes of Scripture in Luke-Acts: Telling the Story of God's People Intertextually.* London: T & T Clark, 2005.

———. "Israel's Prophets Meet Athens' Philosophers: Scriptural Echoes in Acts 17,22-31." *Biblica* 85 (2004): 199-216.

Machen, J. Gresham. "Christianity and Culture." *Princeton Theological Review* 11 (1913).

Marshall, I. Howard. *Acts: An Introduction and Commentary.* Tyndale New Testament Commentary 5. Downers Grove, IL: IVP Academic, 2008.

———. *Luke: Historian and Theologian.* Rev. ed. Downers Grove, IL: InterVarsity Press, 1998.

Martin, Ralph P. *Acts.* Grand Rapids: Eerdmans, 1967.

Maxwell, Kathy. *Hearing Between the Lines: The Audience as Fellow-Worker in Luke-Acts and Its Literary Milieu.* London: T & T Clark, 2010.

Miller, Donald. *Blue Like Jazz.* Nashville: Thomas Nelson, 2003.

Moreland, J. P. *Love Your God with All Your Mind.* Colorado Springs: NavPress, 1997.

———. *The Recalcitrant Imago Dei: Human Persons and the Failure of Naturalism.* London: SCM Press, 2009.

Murphy-O'Connor, Jerome. *Paul: A Critical Life.* Oxford: Oxford University Press, 1996.

Nagel, Thomas. *The Last Word.* New York: Oxford University Press, 1997.

Noll, Mark. *The Scandal of the Evangelical Mind.* Grand Rapids: Eerdmans, 1995.

Oppenheimer, J. Robert. "On Science and Culture." *Encounter* 19 (October 1962): 3-10.

Ordway, Holly. *Not God's Type: A Rational Academic Finds a Radical Faith.* Chicago: Moody Press, 2010.

Orr, D. P., M. Beiter and G. Ingersoll. "Premature Sexual Activity as an Indicator of Psychological Risk." *Pediatrics* 87 (February 1991): 141-47.

Pao, David. *Acts and the Isaianic New Exodus.* Grand Rapids: Baker Academic, 2002.

Pelikan, Jaroslav. *The Emergence of the Catholic Tradition.* Chicago: University of Chicago Press, 1971.

———. *Jesus Through the Centuries.* New York: Harper & Row, 1987.

Penner, Todd. *In Praise of Christian Origins: Stephen and the Hellenists in Lukan Apologetic Historiography.* London: T & T Clark, 2004.

Peterson, David G. *The Acts of the Apostles.* Pillar New Testament Commentary. Grand Rapids: Eerdmans, 2009.

Plantinga, Alvin. *Where the Conflict Really Lies.* New York: Oxford University Press, 2012.

Polhill, John B. *Acts.* New American Commentary 26. Nashville: B & H Academic, 1992.

Post, John. *Metaphysics: A Contemporary Introduction.* New York: Paragon House, 1991.

Postman, Neil. *Amusing Ourselves to Death.* 2nd ed. New York: Penguin, 2005.

Quintilian. *The Instituto Oratoria of Quintilian, with an English Translation.* Translated by H. E. Butler. 4 vols. Cambridge, MA: Harvard University Press, 1953.

Ramsay, William. *St. Paul the Traveller and the Roman Citizen.* London: Hodder & Stoughton, 1892.

Ratzsch, Del. *Philosophy of Science*. Downers Grove, IL: InterVarsity Press, 1986.

Rorty, Richard. *Philosophy and the Mirror of Nature*. Princeton: Princeton University Press, 1979.

Rowe, C. Kavin. *World Upside Down: Reading Acts in the Greco-Roman Age*. Oxford: Oxford University Press, 2009.

Sabom, Michael. *Light and Death*. Grand Rapids: Zondervan, 1998.

Schwartz, Jeffrey M., and Beverly Beyette. *Brain Lock: Free Yourself from Obsessive-Compulsive Disorder*. New York: Harper Perennial, 2007.

Sharp, Mary Jo. "Does the Story of Jesus Mimic Pagan Mystery Stories?" In *Come Let Us Reason*, edited by Paul Copan and William Lane Craig, pp. 151-68. Nashville: B & H Academic, 2012.

Sowell, Thomas. *Intellectuals and Society*. New York: Basic Books, 2012.

Stark, Rodney. *The Victory of Reason*. New York: Random House, 2005.

Thiselton, Anthony. "Realized Eschatology at Corinth." *New Testament Studies* 24 (July 1978): 510-26.

Verschuuren, Gerard M. *What Makes You Tick? A New Paradigm for Neuroscience*. Antioch, CA: Solas Press, 2012.

Volf, Miroslav. *Free of Charge: Giving and Forgiving in a Culture Stripped of Grace*. Grand Rapids: Zondervan, 2006.

Whitehead, Alfred North. *Science and the Modern World*. New York: Mentor, 1952.

Wiker, Benjamin. *Moral Darwinism: How We Became Hedonists*. Downers Grove, IL: InterVarsity Press, 2002.

Williams, Clifford. *Existential Reasons for Belief in God*. Downers Grove, IL: Inter-Varsity Press, 2011.

Winter, Bruce. *After Paul Left Corinth: The Influence of Secular Ethics and Social Change*. Grand Rapids: Eerdmans, 2001.

———. "In Public and in Private: Early Christians and Religious Pluralism." In *One God, One Lord: Christianity in a World of Religious Pluralism*, edited by Andrew D. Clarke and Bruce W. Winter, pp. 125-48. Grand Rapids: Baker Books, 1992.

———. "Introducing the Athenians to God: Paul's Failed Apologetic in Acts 17." *Themelios* 31, no. 1 (2005): 38-59.

Witherington, Ben III. *The Acts of the Apostles: A Socio-Rhetorical Commentary*. Grand Rapids: Eerdmans, 1998.

———. *Paul's Narrative Thought World*. Louisville, KY: Westminster John Knox, 1994.

Wright, N. T. *After You Believe: Why Christian Character Matters*. New York: HarperOne, 2010.

————. "Jesus and the Identity of God." *Ex Auditu* 14 (1998): 42-56.

————. *Paul in Fresh Perspective.* Minneapolis: Fortress, 2005.

————. *The Resurrection of the Son of God.* Minneapolis: Fortress, 2003.

————. *What Saint Paul Really Said.* Grand Rapids: Eerdmans, 1997.

IMAGE CREDITS

Figure 1.1. Asclepius: Baker Photo Archive courtesy of the Altes Museum, Berlin

Figure 2.1. Mars: Kim Walton courtesy of the Capitoline Museum, Rome

Figure 2.2. Mars Hill: Kim Walton

Figure 3.1. Paul's Second Missionary Journey. From *Rediscovering Paul*. ©2011 by Jordan Capes. Used by permission.

Figure 3.2. Athena: Kim Walton courtesy of the Louvre

Figure 3.3. Epicurus: Kim Walton courtesy of the Altes Museum, Berlin

Figure 4.1. Tarsus: Baker Photo Archive

Figure 4.2. Socrates: Kim Walton courtesy of the British Museum

Figure 4.3. Augustine by Antonello da Messina: The Yorck Project / Wikimedia Commons

Figure 4.4. Fred Hoyle: Donald D. Clayton / AIP Emilio Segre Visual Archives, Clayton Collection

Figure 4.5. Nietzsche: Library of Congress, Prints & Photographs Division (reproduction number LC-DIG-ggbain-17575)

Figure 4.6. Galileo: Library of Congress, Prints & Photographs Division (reproduction number LC-USZ62-7923)

Figure 5.1. Troas: Baker Photo Archive

Figure 5.2. Corinth bema: Kim Walton

Figure 6.1. Antiochus IV Epiphanes: Kim Walton courtesy of the Eretz Israel Museum

Figure 6.2. Agora: Kim Walton

Figure 6.3. Galilee tomb: Baker Photo Archive

Figure 6.4. Thessaloniki theater: Kim Walton

Figure 7.1. Mukhraqa monastery: Baker Photo Archive

Figure 7.2. Artemis: Kim Walton courtesy of the National Archaeological Museum of Athens

Figure 7.3. Church of the Holy Sepulcher: Kim Walton

Figure 8.1. Cicero: Baker Photo Archive courtesy of the Vatican Museum

Figure 8.2. Agora and Mars Hill: Kim Walton

Figure 8.3. Temple to Zeus: Kim Walton

Figure 10.1. Altar: Kim Walton courtesy of the Palatine Museum, Rome

Finding the Textbook You Need

The IVP Academic Textbook Selector
is an online tool for instantly finding the IVP books
suitable for over 250 courses across 24 disciplines.

---

www.ivpress.com/academic/textbookselector